SAMSUNG GALAXY TAB S FOR SENIORS

A RIDICULOUSLY SIMPLE GUIDE TO THE NEXT GENERATION OF SAMSUNG GALAXY TABLETS

SCOTT LA COUNTE

RIDICULOUSLY
SIMPLE BOOKS

ANAHEIM, CALIFORNIA

www.RidiculouslySimpleBooks.com

Disclaimer: *Please note, while every effort has been made to ensure accuracy, this book is not endorsed by Samsung, Inc. and should be considered unofficial.*

Table of Contents

INTRODUCTION

The Galaxy is a powerful tablet. I'm sure you are excited to get the most out of it. But what if your all new to this tablet thing? Or maybe you've used tablets before, but not one made by Samsung—the iPad, for instance. This guide has you covered!

If you are looking for something comprehensive--that tells you how to side load apps and do things the average person who never do, then keep looking. But if you need something that will help you get started, then read on!

Inside, you'll learn about:

- What makes Galaxy different from iOS, Android, and other smartphones
- Setting up your tablet
- Installing apps
- Accessibility features
- Using the camera
- Surfing the Internet
- Changing system settings
- And much more!

[1]

START HERE

This chapter will cover:
- Different tablets
- Setup

WHAT A DIFFERENCE A TABLET MAKES

When it comes to Android there are a lot of tablets—like hundreds of them. Samsung, however, makes things slightly easier on consumers by only having two main choices. The Tab S series and the Tab A series. They typically release one model in each series every year. In 2020, the models were the Tab A7 (in 8.4in and 10.4in size screens) and the Tab S7 (and S7+, which is the same model but bigger screen).

Samsung builds there tablets using Android OS (the latest build as of this writing is Android 10), but they put a unique UI on top of it (it's called the One UI, and as of this writing, tablets have One UI 2).

So what's the difference between the A and S series? A series are lower end and ideal for casual web browsers; S series are for more professional years who need more power. The body of the tablets are pretty similar--although the S7 does have a slightly more edge-to-edge display; it's the inside where you really start seeing the difference. The S7 is faster, tends to get better battery life, has a better camera, more RAM, better screen resolution, and larger internal memory. The S7 is also about twice the price of the series A tablets.

There's nothing particularly wrong with the A series tablet. They may not have the same power, but they can still do a lot. If all you want to do is use the tablet on the couch to read a book or magazine, or browse Facebook, then it's perfect for you; if you plan on installing large, memory intensive apps, then the S series will probably better for you.

SETUP

The setup is pretty intuitive, but there are still screens that might confuse you a little. If you are a self-starter and like to just try things, then skip to the next section (Finding Your Way Around) on the main UI elements of Samsung. If you want a more thorough walk-through, then read away!

Samsung knows you want to get started using your tablet, so they've made the process pretty quick; most people will spend about 10 or 15 minutes.

The first thing you'll see is the "Let's go!" screen. There's also an accessibly option, which will let you turn on adaptive controls if you are visually or hearing impaired. When you are ready to get started, tap the blue arrow button.

Next up are the terms. You have to agree to them before continuing. There's a lot of them, so make sure and set aside a few hours in your day to read everything...or just be like 99.9999% of people and just check them all off and tap Next.

Once you go through all the terms, then it will ask you for your wi-fi. You'll notice on the bottom there's a back arrow and a skip. These options will be on almost all the setup screens. Back takes you to the previous step. And skip takes you to the next area of setup. If you skip, then Samsung will not be able to check for updates (chances are there will be one), so if you want your tablet running as smooth as possibly, I recommend you don't skip it.

Choose a Wi–Fi network

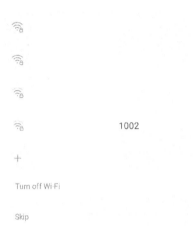

Once you find your wi-fi, you'll see a screen that says it's looking for updates. It might take a few minutes, so be patient.

Checking for updates...
This may take a few minutes

After the updates, it's time to log into your Google Account. Don't have one? It's free—just tap that Create Account option. You can skip this step, but again, I don't recommend it. It's going to do two important things:

1. If you have Gmail, you'll be able to check it on your tablet by setting up your account (as

well as Google Apps—like Google Drive, Google Docs, etc.).

2. You'll probably want to install apps. To install apps, you need the Google Play Store and a Google Account.

Google

Sign in

with your Google Account. Learn more

Email or phone

Forgot email?

Create account

If you skip any of these steps, you'll be able to add them in later—so if you're unsure, then don't feel pressured.

If you do add your Google Account, then guess what? Even more terms!

We publish the Google Terms of Service so that you know what to expect as you use our services. By clicking 'I Agree,' you agree to these terms.

You are also agreeing to the Google Play Terms of Service to enable discovery and management of apps.

And remember, the Google Privacy Policy describes how Google handles information generated as you use Google services. You can always visit your Google Account (account.google.com) to take a Privacy Checkup or to adjust your privacy controls.

Don't add this account now   I agree

The next step is restoring from a backup. If you have another tablet or Android device with the same Google account, then you might see it here. If you've never had anything Android, then there's nothing to restore from. If you choose to restore, then it will put the same settings, apps, and contacts on your device. It probably won't be a mirror image of that device, but you'll notice a lot of similarities.

Choose a backup to restore

SM-
11 hours ago, 6:01 AM

Don't restore

The next option is to restore from Google Services; even if you aren't accessing it often, chances are you've used it before—or someone has shared content from it.

Samsung has a lot of options when it comes to protecting your tablet. Unlike many phones, there's no fingerprint sensor, but there's plenty of other options such as, facial recognition, pattern (meaning you swipe a certain way to unlock your tablet), pin number, or password.

In case you aren't sure what any of this means, whenever you open your tablet, if you pick protection, it will be locked; nobody can open your tablet without the protection you pick. This may not be a big deal, but I still recommend it—if you ever mistakenly leave your tablet anywhere, it ensures someone can't access sensitive information.

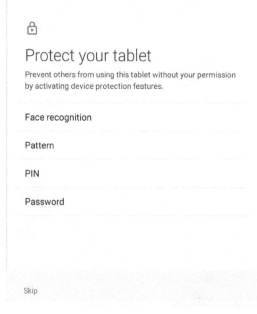

The most secure protection is facial recognition. That means whenever you want to unlock your tablet, you just hold it to your pretty face and it opens.

You'll also need to set up another password. So if you are ever in a place where you can't use your face (the lighting is too bad, for example), you'll still be able to access your tablet.

In case you're sitting there saying "But what if I wear glasses?" that's the next step! If you wear glasses, then make sure you put them on.

Do you wear glasses?

If you do, put them on now so you can register your face both with glasses and without them.

○ Yes

◉ No

If you want to transfer content from your old device like photos, then that's the next step. What if it was a non-Android device (i.e. the iPad)? Doesn't matter! Even if it's an iPad, you can do this.

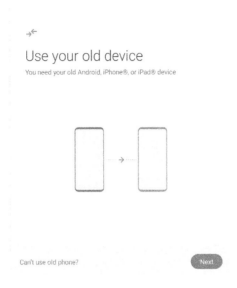

Use your old device

You need your old Android, iPhone®, or iPad® device

Can't use old phone?   Next

Are you absolutely loving all these login screens and pages and pages of legal terms and conditions? Good! Because there's more! Next up is signing into your Samsung account. Again, don't have one, then sign up free.

Signing in or signing up for a Samsung account is going to help you find your tablet if it goes missing and use Samsung exclusive services. I recommend doing it. You can also sign in with Google.

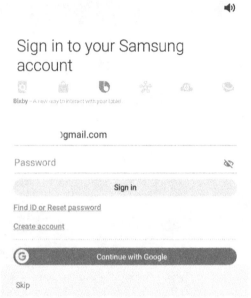

Once you're done, you'll finally see a screen that says finished, and it's time to start using your tablet!

[3]
OVERVIEW

This chapter will cover:
- Exploring the Samsung UI
- Notification bar
- Edge bar
- Gestures

FINDING YOUR WAY AROUND

People come to the Samsung from all sorts of different places: iPad, other Android tablets, flip phone, two Styrofoam cups tied together with string. This next section is a crash course in the interface. If you've used Android before, then it might seem a little simple, so skip ahead if you already know all of this.

If any of this seems a little rushed, there's good reason: it is! We'll cover these points in more detail later. This is just a quick starter / reference.

When you see your main screen for the first time, you will see six components. They are (from top to bottom): the Notification Bar, Add Weather Widget, Google Search App, Short Cuts Icons, Favorites Bar, navigation.

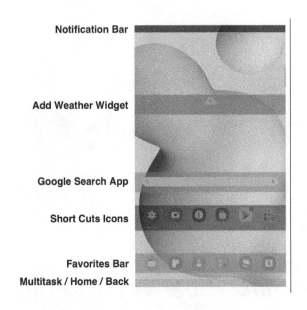

Notification Bar

Add Weather Widget

Google Search App

Short Cuts Icons

Favorites Bar
Multitask / Home / Back

- **Notifications Bar** - This is a pull-down menu (slide down to expand it) and it's where you'll see all your alerts (new email or text, for example) and where you can go to change settings quickly.
- **Add Weather Widget** – Widgets are like mini apps that display information on your screen; weather is what's shown here, but they can be anything from Gmail, to calendars, and hundreds of things in between.

- **Google Search App** – The Google Search app is another example of a widget. As the name implies, it can search Google for information; but it also searches apps on your tablet.
- **Short Cuts Icons** – These are apps that you frequently use and want quick access to.
- **Favorites Bar** – These are like short cuts, except you see them on all your screens. You can add whatever you want to this area, but these are the apps Samsung thinks you'll use most.
- **Navigation Bar** – These are shortcuts for getting around your tablet: the first is the multi-task button, which helps you quickly switch apps; the next is the Home button which gets you back to the Home screen; and the last is the back button, which returns you to the previous screen.

NOTIFICATIONS BAR

Next to the short cut bar, the area you'll use the most is the notification bar. This is where you'll get, you guessed it, notifications! What's a notification? That's any kind of notice you have elected to receive. A few examples: text message alerts, email alerts, amber alerts, and apps that have updates.

When you drag your finger down from the notification bar, you'll get a list of several settings that you can adjust. Press and hold any of these options and you'll open an app with even more options.

From right to left these are the options you can change or use:

- Wi-fi
- Sound (tap to mute sounds)
- Bluetooth
- Lock the device from auto-rotating
- Airplane mode (which turns off wi-fi and Bluetooth)
- Power saving mode (which limits the speed of the tablets CPU and decreases the screen brightness to increase the battery life.
- QR Code scanner
- Blue light filter (turning this on can help you sleep better at night, as blue light before bed has been known to affect sleeping habits).

If you continue dragging down, this thin menu expands and there are a few more options.

The first is at the bottom of the screen—it's the slider, and it makes your device brighter or dimmer depending on which way you drag it.

Above that, there are several controls. Many of these controls are just an on / off toggle, but some let you long press to see expanded options. Some will be more obvious that others, but I'll go through each one quickly, starting from top left.

- Wi-Fi – Tap to turn off Wi-Fi; long press to change networks and see Wi-Fi settings.
- Sound – Tap to turn off sound; long press to see sound settings.

- Bluetooth – Turns off Bluetooth; long press to connect to a device or see Bluetooth settings.
- Autorotate – Tapping will lock the device orientation, so if you turn the device the screen will not rotate.
- Airplane mode – turns off features like Wi-Fi, cellular, and Bluetooth.
- Power mode – turns on a power saving mode that will help your tablet last longer; if you are low on batteries and not near a charger, this will help you get a little more life out of your tablet. Long pressing it will bring up expanded power save features.
- Scan QR Code – QR codes aren't as used today, but occasionally you might see a paper or flier with a box that you can scan. This is a QR code; when you use your camera to scan it, it will take you to a website.
- Blue light filter – Toggling on will turn off the blue light on your tablet; it gives your tablet a more brownish hue. Looking at a blue light can make it difficult to sleep, so it's recommended to turn this on at night.
- Location – Toggling this on / off lets apps see your location; for example, if you are using a map for driving directions, it gives the app permission to see where

you are located. Long pressing will show expanded location settings.

- Smart view – lets you mirror your screen (or sound) to other devices (such as a Google Home).
- Do not disturb – Turns off notifications so you don't receive messages or tablet calls (they'll go straight to voice mail); long pressing expands Do not disturb settings.
- Secure folder – Creates a secure folder for your devices, so you can password protect certain apps and documents.
- Screen recorder – This option lets you create a video of what's on your screen; you can create a tutorial for something or even record a game. Long pressing will show expanded settings.
- Quick share – This option lets you wirelessly share photos, videos and other files with another device. Long pressing will show expanded settings.
- Sync – Sync docs and photos with other devices.

If you swipe you will see even more options to pick from.

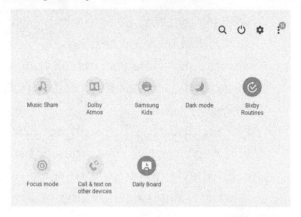

- Music share – Shares music that you are listening to, so you can listen together. Long pressing will show expanded settings.
- Dolby Amos – Toggling on will give your device superior Dolby Amos sound. Long pressing will show expanded settings.
- Samsung kids – Turns on kids mode, which gives your device a kid-friendly UI and turns off several apps.
- Dark mode – Gives menus and some apps a black background instead of white. Long pressing will show expanded settings.
- Bixby routines – Sets up Bixby. Long pressing will show expanded settings.
- Focus mode – Lets you set timers and turn off certain apps for a period of time to give you a more distraction-free experience. Long pressing will show expanded settings.

- Call & Text other devices – Let's you sync your tablet with your phone to text and call people.
- Daily Board – toggles the Daily Board on / off; this shows a recap of your day when you are not using your tablet.

On the notification area you'll also see two op-tions for Media and Devices.

Media lets you control music and videos on other devices.

Take control of music and videos playing on your tablet as well as other Samsung devices. You can also switch playback to another device without missing a moment.
View more

Devices lets you connect to devices using Blue-tooth and see what devices you are already con-nected to.

Access the SmartThings devices and scenes you use most often directly from the quick panel. You can also add devices that are connected directly to your tablet, such as Bluetooth devices.

Up on top is a handful of other controls.

The config button brings up expanded settings for your tablet.

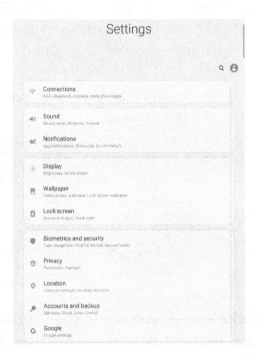

The power button will let you restart or power down your device.

GETTING AROUND QUICKLY

As mentioned, the bottom of the screen is your navigation area for getting around.

This is nice, but better is setting up gestures to handle navigating around your tablet. This will turn this section off to give a tad more screen real estate.

To change it, swipe up from the bottom of your screen (this will bring up all your apps), then tap Settings. Next, go to the Display option.

In Display options, scroll down until you get to Navigation bar, and then tap it.

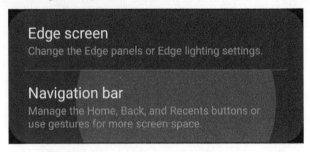

In the Navigation bar menu, select Full screen gestures.

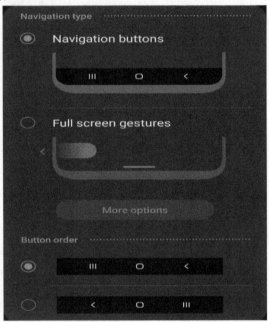

Nice! It's gone! But what are the gestures?! Before you leave settings, it will give you a little preview of how they work, but below is a recap:

- Swipe up and release to get to your Home screen from any app.

- Swipe up and hold to bring up multitasking.
- Swipe right or left from the bottom edge of your screen to go backwards and forward.

You might recall that swiping up from the bottom showed you all your apps. That gesture now returns to the Home screen, so how do you see all your apps? From your Home screen, swipe up in the middle of the screen to see them.

When it comes to getting around your Samsung, learning how to use gestures will be the quickest, most effective method. You can change some of the gesture options by going to System > Advanced features > Motion and gestures.

The most important gesture is how to get back to the Home screen—there are no buttons after all. That's the easiest one to remember: swipe up from the bottom of the screen.

MULTITASKING

Those are the easy gestures to remember; if you want to move around quickly, however, you need to know the two big multitask gestures, which help you switch between apps.

The first is to see your open apps. To do this, swipe up like you're going to the Home screen, but keep going until about the middle of the screen and then stop and lift your finger—don't make a quick swipe-up gesture like you would when going Home. This will show you previews of all of your open apps, and you can swipe between them. Tap the one you want to open.

The quickest way to switch back and forth between two or three apps, however, is to swipe from left to right along the bottom edge of the screen. This swipes between apps in the order that you have used them.

ZOOM

Need to see text bigger? There are two ways to do that. Note: this works on many, but not all apps.

The first way is to pinch to zoom.

r with the Additic
: between you an
es. It is importan
Collectively, this l
s".

etween what the
al Terms say, the
elation to that Se

The second way is to double tap on the text.

ROTATE

You probably have noticed if you rotate your tablet, it rotates the screen. What if you don't want to rotate the entire screen? You can turn that off very easily. Swipe down and then tap the "arrows" button to enable or disable it.

EDGE BAR

One of the features that has always stood out on Samsung devices is the way they make use of all areas of your tablet...right up to the edge.

The Edge bar brings up short cut menus quickly no matter where you are on the tablet. To access it, swipe left from the side of your screen near the top; the Edge bar outline can just barely be seen on your Home screen. It's right next to the down volume button and extends just above the up volume button.

Swiping right brings up a side menu.

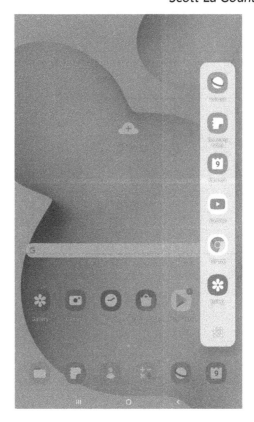

On the bottom left corner, you can click the bulleted list icon to see all of your Edge bar menus.

Swiping right and left lets you toggle between them.

Clicking on the config icon on the bottom left corner will let you select and deselect the Edge bar menus that are shown.

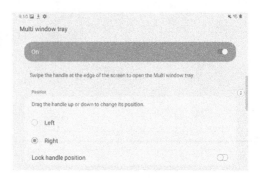

To add an app to the App Edge bar menu, just tap the pencil icon. You can drag any app into that empty box; remove an app if you'd like to add more.

To remove an app, tap and hold the icon, then drag it to remove.

[4]

GETTING PERSONAL

This chapter will cover:
- Customizing screens
- Split screens
- Gestures

MAKING PRETTY SCREENS

If you've used an iPhone or iPad, then you may notice the screen looks a little...bare. There are only a few buttons on it. Maybe you like that. If so, then good for you! Skip ahead. If you want to decorate that screen with shortcuts and widgets, then read on.

ADDING SHORTCUTS

Any app you want on this screen, just find it and then press and hold; when a menu comes up, drag it upward until the screen appears and move it to where you want it to go.

To remove an app from a screen, tap and hold, then tap Remove from the pop-up box.

WIDGETS

Shortcuts are nice, but widgets are better. Widgets are sort of like mini-programs that run on your screen. A common widget people put on their screen is the weather forecast. Throughout the day the widget will update automatically with up-to-date info.

It's such a popular widget that Samsung has put the option on your Home screen and you only have to tap it to set it up.

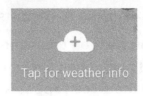

Once you add your city, it's going to automatically start showing. Clicking on it will open up the app.

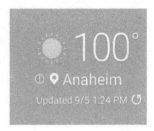

Weather is nice, but there are lots of widgets you can add to your Home screen. How do you get them? Press and hold your finger on the middle of the screen. This brings up the Home screen options menu. Tap the Widgets icon.

This will show you the most popular widgets, but if you know what you want, then just search for it.

For this example, I searched for Gmail, who I know has a widget. I tap it, then it let's me select where I want it on the screen.

When you tap on the widget, you'll notice little dots on the side. That lets you make it bigger or smaller. Just drag it to your ideal width and height.

To remove any widget, just tap and hold it. From the pop-up, tap Remove from Home.

WALLPAPER

Adding wallpaper to your screen is done in a similar way. Tap and hold your finger on the Home screen, when the menu comes up, select Wallpaper instead of Widgets.

From the Wallpapers menu you have a few choices:

- My wallpapers – These are wallpapers you have purchased or ones that Samsung pre-loads.
- Gallery – Pictures you've taken.

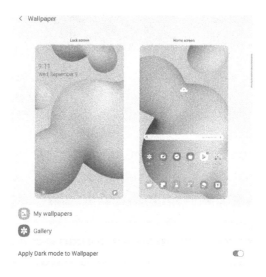

SAMSUNG DAILY

Samsung Daily is sort of like a recap of your day and daily recommendations for things to download. You can see it by swiping left from your Home screen.

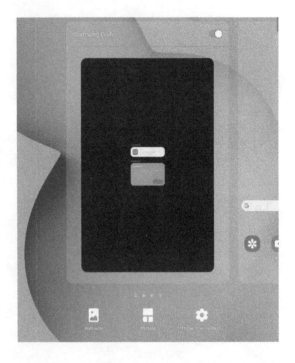

It's not the worst feature on the tablet, but a lot of people don't really see value in it. If you'd rather not see it, then tap and hold on your Home screen, then swipe left when you see the Home options. On the Samsung Daily preview, toggle the switch to off.

ADDING SCREENS

Adding screens for even more shortcuts and widgets is easy. Tap and hold the Home screen, and swipe to the right.

Next, click the + icon which will add a screen. When you return to your Home screen, you can swipe right and start adding shortcuts and widgets to it.

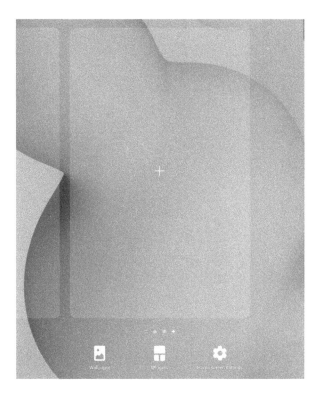

HOME SCREEN SETTINGS

To access even more Home screen settings, tap and hold the Home screen, then tap the config Home screen settings icon.

The first area that you'll probably want to change is the Home screen layout.

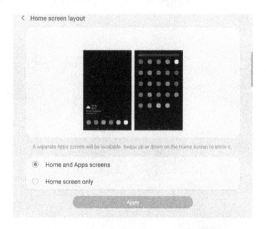

The Home screen grid is also useful if you want to get a little more use out of the screen real estate; it adjusts icon size / placement to fit more or fewer icons on the screen.

The rest of the settings are just toggle switches.

A WORD, OR TWO, ABOUT MENUS

It's pretty intuitive that if you tap on an icon, it opens the app. What's not so obvious is if you tap and hold there are other options. Every app is different. Usually, they're shortcuts—tapping and holding over the Tablet icon, for example, brings up your favorites; doing the same thing over the camera brings up a selfie mode shortcut. Tap and hold over your favorite apps to see what shortcuts are available.

SPLIT SCREENS

The Samsung tablet comes in different sizes; a bigger screen obviously gives you a lot more space, which makes split screen apps a pretty handy feature. It works on the smaller Samsung as well, though it doesn't feel as effective on the smaller screen.

To use this feature, swipe up to bring up multitasking; next, tap the icon above the window you want to turn into split screen (note: this feature is not supported on all apps); if split screen is available, you'll see a menu that has an option for split screen.

Once you tap split screen, it will let you swipe left and right to find the app you want to split the screen with. Tap the one you want.

Your screen is now split in two.

That thin blue bar in the middle is adjustable; you can move it up or down so one of the apps has more screen real estate.

To exit this mode, drag the black bar either all the way to the top or all the way to the bottom until one of the apps completely goes away.

[5]
THE BASICS

This chapter will cover:
- Sending messages
- Finding and downloading apps
- Driving directions

Now that you have your tablet set up and know your way around the device at its most basic level, let's go over the apps you'll be using the most.

Before we get into it, there's something you need to know: how to open apps not on your Home screen. It's easy. From your Home screen, swipe up from the middle of the screen. Notice that menu that's appearing? That's where all the additional apps are.

CONTACTS

Let's open up the Contacts app to get started. See it? It's on your favorites bar, but you can also swipe up to see all your apps and get to it.

It looks like this:

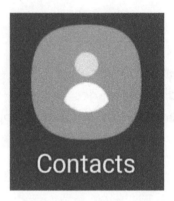

Chances are if you've added your email account, you'll already have a lot of contacts listed. Like hundreds! There's going to be a message about merging them—that's up to you.

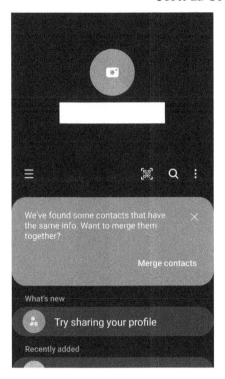

You can either search for the contact by clicking the magnifying glass, scroll slowly, or head to the right-hand side of the app and scroll—this lets you quickly scroll by letters. Just slide your finger until you see the letter of the contact you want and then stop.

I'm getting ahead of myself, however! Before you can scroll, it would be nice to know how to add a contact so there are people to scroll to. To add a contact, tap on that plus sign.

Before adding the contact, it will ask you where you want it saved—your Samsung account, the tablet or Google. It's entirely up to you, but saving it to Google might save you some trouble if you switch to a different tablet manufacturer in the future.

Adding a person looks more like applying for a job than adding a contact. There are rows and rows of fields!

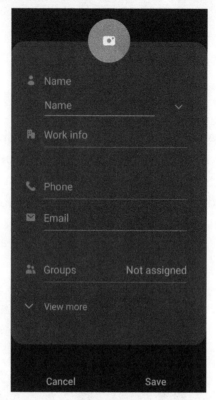

Just in case you weren't overwhelmed by all the fields, you can tap more fields and get even more!

Here's the most important thing you need to know: fields are optional! You can add a name and email and that's it. You don't even have to add their tablet number. If you want to call them, then that would certainly help though.

If you have a hard time remembering who people are, then you can also take a picture or add a picture you already have. Comes in handy if you have eight kids and you can't remember if Joey is the one with blonde hair or red hair. Just tap the camera icon up top, then tap either Gallery (to assign a photo you've already taken) or Camera (to take a picture of them); you can also use one of the avatar type icons Samsung has.

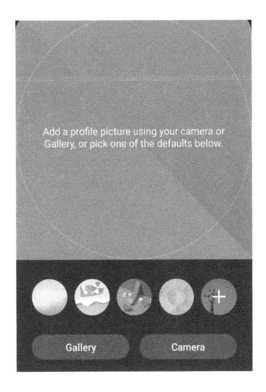

Once you are done, tap the save button.

EDITING A CONTACT

If you add an email and then later decide you should add a tablet number, or if you want to edit anything else, then just find the name in your contacts and tap it once. This brings up all the info you've already added.

Go to the bottom of the screen and tap on the Edit option button. This makes the contact editable. Go to your desired field and update. When you are finished make sure to tap Save.

SHARING A CONTACT

If you have your tablet long enough, someone will ask you for so-and-so's tablet number. The old-fashioned way was to write it down. But you have a tablet, so you aren't old-fashioned!

The new way to share a number is to find the person in your contacts, tap their name, then tap Share on the bottom left corner of the screen.

From here you have a few options, but the easiest is to text or email the contact to your friend. This sends them a contact card. So if you have other information with that contact (such as email) then that will be sent over as well.

DELETE CONTACT

Deleting a contact is the same as sharing a contact. The only difference is once you tap their name, you tap the delete icon to the right (not the share to the left). This erases them from your tablet, but not your life.

GET ORGANIZED

Once you start getting lots of contacts, then it's going to make finding someone more time-consuming. Groups helps. You can add a Group for "Family" for instance, and then stick all of your family members there.

When you open your contacts and tap those three lines in the upper left corner, you'll see a menu. This is where you'll see your Groups. So with Groups, you can jump right into that list and find the contact you need.

You can also send the entire group inside the Group an email or text message. So for instance, if your child is turning two and you want to remind everyone in your "Family" contact not to come, then just tap on that Group.

But what if you don't have labels? Or if you want to add people to a label? Easy. Remember that long application you used to add a contact? One of the fields was called "Groups." You have to tap more to see it. It's all the way at the bottom. One of the last fields, in fact.

If you've never added a label or want to add a new one, then just start typing. If you have another one that you'd like to use, then just tap the arrow and select it.

When you are done, don't forget to tap Save.

You can also quickly assign someone to a group by tapping on the contact's name, then selecting Create Group from the upper right.

Once you tap that, you'll get to add a name, assign a ringtone, and assign other members.

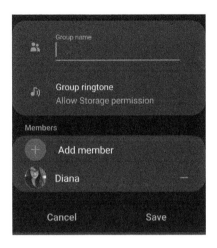

DELETE GROUP

If you decide you no longer want to have a label, then just go to the menu I showed you above—side menu, then the three dots. From here, tap the Delete Group.

If there's just one person you want to boot from the label, then tap them and go to the Group and delete it.

MAKING CALLS

Assuming you have sync-d your tablet to your phone, you can also make calls and messages on your device.

This section will walk you through it, but if it's not working on your device, remember: you must sync your tablet to a phone.

You can make a call by opening the Contacts app, then selecting the contact, and then tapping on their tablet number. Alternatively, you can tap on the Tablet button from your Home screen or favorite bar.

There are a few options when you open this app. Let's talk about each one.

Starting from the far left is the Keypad tab. It's green because you are already there.

In the middle is the Recents tab. If you've made any calls, they'll show here.

The last option is Contacts, which opens a version of the Contacts app that's within the Tablet app.

If you want to dial someone the old-fashioned way by tapping in numbers, then tap them, and tap the call icon. You can also tap the video icon to start a video call.

When you are done with the call, hit the End button on your tablet.

ANSWER AND DECLINE CALLS

What do you do when someone calls you? Probably ignore it because it's a telemarketer!

It's easy to accept a call, however. When the tablet rings, the number will appear and if the person is in your Contacts, then the name will appear as well. To answer, just swipe the "answer." To decline just drag the "decline."

PHONE SETTINGS

If you haven't noticed already, there are settings for pretty much everything. Samsung is a *highly* customizable tablet. To get to settings, go to the upper right corner, then select Settings.

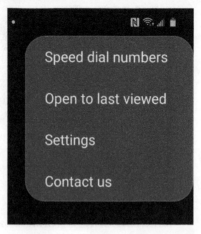

From settings you can set up ringtones, add numbers to block, set up your voicemail and much more.

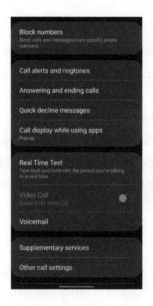

PLAY ANGRY BIRDS WHILE TALKING TO ANGRY MOM

What if you're on a call with your mom and she's just complaining about something, but you don't want to be rude and hang up? Easy. You multitask! This means you could play Angry Birds while talking!

To multitask, just swipe up from the bottom of your tablet and open the app you want to work in while you are talking. The call will show in the notification area. Tap it to return to the call.

MESSAGES

Now that you know how Contacts and the Tablet works, messaging will be like second nature. They share many of the same properties.

Let's open up the Messages app (you have to swipe up and go to all apps). It looks like this:

CREATE / SEND A MESSAGE

When you have selected the contact(s) to send a message to, tap Compose. You can also manually type in the number in the text field.

You can add more than one contact—this is known as a group text.

The first time you send a message, it's going to probably look pretty bare like the image below. Assuming you have never sent one, it's going to be blank. Once you start getting messages, you can tap on New category to create labels for them—so all your family messages, for example, will be in one place.

Once you are ready to send your first message, tap the message icon.

The top field is where you put who it's going to (or the group name if it's several people). You can use the + icon to find people in your contacts.

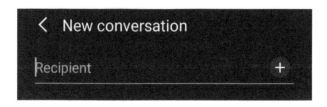

Use the text field to type out your message.

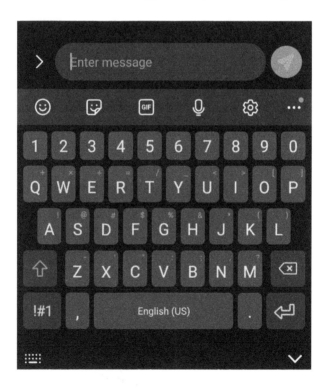

It looks pretty basic, but there's actually a *lot* here. Starting on the bottom, there's a little keyboard—that's to switch to a different type of keyboard; to the right of that is a down arrow, which will collapse the keyboard. To get it back, just click the message box again.

Just above the keyboard icon, is a !#1 button, which will switch the alpha keyboard to a numeric / symbol keyboard (so you have quick access to symbols like @, ?, %).

Typing in another language or need an accent sign? Long press the letter and you'll reveal more characters and symbols for that letter.

Finally, at the top is a set of six additional icons.

From left to right, the first is the Emoji pack. If you want to respond to someone with an Emoji, then that's what you tap.

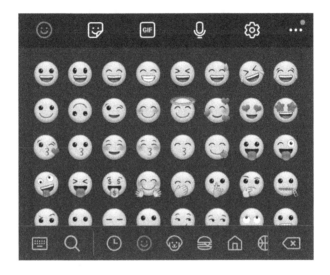

You can scroll through all of them by swiping right, but because there's so many of them, they are also grouped together, and you can jump to a group by tapping on the associated image on the bottom.

Next to the Emoji icon is the Bitmoji sticker icon. I'll cover Bitmoji later, but for now, let's just say Bitmoji is like an emoji that is customized to look like you. To use it, you have to download it. It's free.

Next is the GIF search; you have to agree to the terms to use it. It's basically a search engine for GIF images; so if you want to find a birthday GIF to put in a message, for example, you could search "birthday" and see literally dozens and dozens of GIFs. If you don't know what a GIF is, they are small images that move on a loop—kind of like mini movies that last a couple seconds.

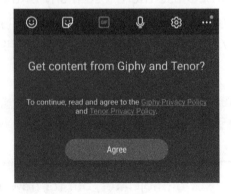

To the right of the GIF icon is the microtablet icon, which lets you record a voice message instead of typing it.

You know Samsung loves its settings, so it probably won't surprise you that the config icon launches keyboard settings.

Because they love settings so much, there are a few more when you tap the three dots; you can adjust the keyboard size here, but also use some of the many other features—such as text editing and translation.

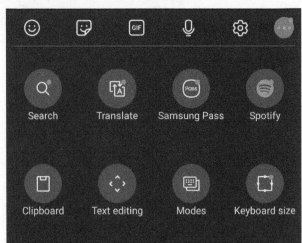

So, like I said, there's a lot to this keyboard. But the keyboard is only half the fun! Look above it…that little > icon will bring out some more things you can do with the message.

There are three additional options. The first is to include a picture that's in your photo gallery.

The next is to either take a photo or record a video.

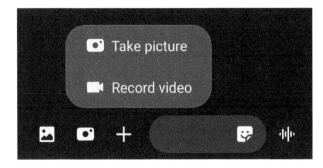

And the last is a series of extra options.

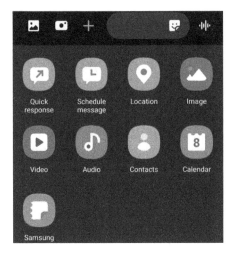

From left to right starting at the top:

- Quick response – Gives a list of common responses so you don't have to type anything.
- Schedule message – Lets you define when the message will be sent.
- Location – Shares where you are currently located with a person. So if a person is meeting you and they're saying

"I'm looking for you, but don't see you!" you can send this to give them a better idea.

- Image / Video – this is similar to adding a video / image from your gallery (you can actually do that here as well), but it also searches for them in other places like Google Drive.
- Audio – Share an audio file.
- Contacts – Share someone's contact information.
- Calendar – Share an event in your calendar with another person.
- Samsung – Share a Samsung Note with a person.

When you are ready to send your message, tap the arrow with the SMS under it.

VIEW MESSAGE

When you get a message, your tablet will vibrate, chirp, or do nothing—it all depends on how you set up your tablet. To view the message, you can either open the app, or swipe down to see your notifications—one will be the text message.

WHERE'S AN APP FOR THAT?

I mentioned earlier that you could play Angry Birds while talking to your angry mom on the tablet. Sound fun? But where is Angry Birds on your tablet? It's not! You have to download it.

Adding and removing apps on the Galaxy is easy. Head to your favorite bar on the bottom of your Home screen and tap the Google Play app.

This launches the Play Store.

From here you can browse the top apps, see editors' picks, look through categories, or, if you have an app in mind, search for it. The Play Store isn't just for apps. You can use the tabs on the top to go to movies, books, and music. Any kind of downloadable content that's offered by Google can be found here.

When you see the app you want, tap on it. You can read through reviews, see screenshots, and install it on your tablet. To install, simply tap the install button—if it's a paid app you'll be prompted to buy it. If there's no price, it's free (or offers in-app payments—which means the app is free, but there are premium features inside it you may have to pay for).

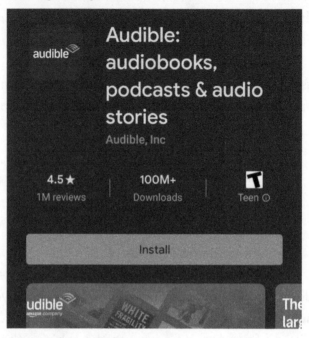

The app is now stored in the app section of your device (remember the section you get to when you swipe up from the bottom to the top?).

REMOVE APP

If you decide you no longer want an app, go to the app in the app menu and tap and hold it. This brings up a box with a few options. The one you want is Uninstall.

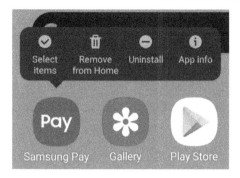

If you downloaded the app from the Play Store, you can always delete it. Some apps that were pre-installed on your tablet cannot be deleted.

DRIVING DIRECTIONS

Back in the day, you may have had a GPS. It was a fancy plastic device that would give you directions for anywhere in North America. You can throw out that device because your tablet is your new GPS...kind of. Kind of because you need to have some way to get data to your tablet if you don't have wi-fi.

To get directions, swipe up to open up your apps, and go to the Google folder. Tap the Maps app.

It's automatically going to be set to wherever you are currently at—which is both creepy and useful.

To get started, just type where you want to go. I'm searching for Disneyland, Anaheim.

It automatically starts filling in what it thinks you are going to type and tells you the distance. When you see the one you want, tap it.

It pinpoints the location on the map and also gives you an option to call, share or get directions to the location. If you want to zoom out or in, just use two fingers and pinch in or out on the screen.

It automatically gets directions from where you are. Want it from a different location? Just tap on the "Your location" field and type where you want to go. You can also reverse the directions by tapping on the double arrows. When you are ready to go, tap Start.

What if you don't want to drive? What if you want to walk? Or bike? Or take a taxi? There are options for all of those and more! Tap the slider under the address bar to whatever you prefer. This updates the directions—when you walk, for example, it will show you one-way streets and also update the time it will take you.

What if you want to drive but are like me: terrified of freeways in California? There's an option to avoid highways. Tap the menu button in the upper right corner of the screen and select Route options (there are actually lots of other things packed in here like adding stops, sharing directions, and sharing your location).

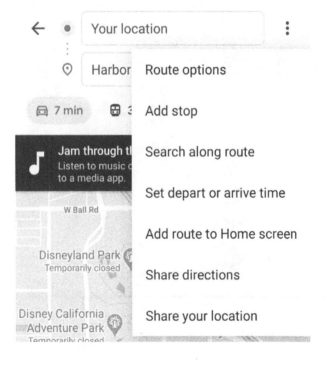

In the Route options, select what you want to avoid, and hit Done. You are now rerouted to a longer route—notice how the times probably changed?

Once you get your directions, you can swipe up to get turn-by-turn directions.

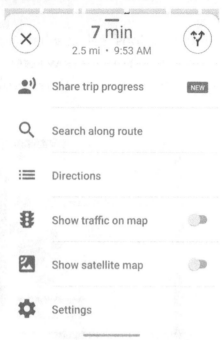

You can even see what it looks like from the street. It's called Street View.

Street View isn't only for streets. Google is expanding the feature everywhere. If you hold your finger over the map, there will be an option to show Street View if it's available. Just tap the thumbnail. Here's a Street View of Disneyland:

You can wander around the entire park! If only you could ride the rides, too! You can get even closer to the action by picking up the Dreamview headset. When you stick your tablet in that, you can turn your head and the view turns with you.

Street View is also available in a lot of malls and other tourist attractions. Point your map to the Smithsonian in Washington, DC and get a pretty cool Street View.

LIVE CAPTIONING

One of the bigger features to Android 10 is live captioning; live captioning can transcribe any video you record and show what's being said. It works surprisingly well and is pretty accurate.

To turn it on, go to Settings > Accessibility > Hearing enhancements > Live caption.

In the settings, you can also toggle off profanity, and, coming soon, select a different language. If it's something you'd only occasionally use, I recommend leaving it toggled off, but having it toggled on under Live Caption in volume control. With that toggled on, all you have to do is press the volume button. Once you do that, you'll see the option to turn it on; it's the bottom option.

Once it's on, you'll start seeing a transcription appear in seconds.

SHARING WI-FI

Anytime you have guests over, you almost always get the question: what's your wi-fi password? If you are like me, then it probably annoys you. Maybe your password is really long, maybe you just don't like giving out your password, or maybe you are just too embarrassed to say that it's "Feet$Fet-ishLover1." Whatever the reason, then you will love sharing your wi-fi with QR codes. Gone are the days of giving this info out. Just give them a code that they scan, and they'll have access without ever knowing what your password is.

To use it, go to your wi-fi settings, then select the Wi-Fi options and Wi-Fi Direct.

Make sure both devices have Wi-Fi on and follow the directions.

SAMSUNG KIDS

One place Samsung truly shines above other companies is with its parental control features and kids mode. Yes, other devices have parental controls, but Samsung takes it up a notch by creating a UI that's just for kids.

With kids mode, you can quickly toggle it on and off for those moments where you need to distract a child.

To access it, swipe down to bring down your notification bar, then swipe right one time. You'll see it in the second row. Tap it.

The first time you launch it, you'll have to download a very small program. It will take a few seconds depending on your connection speed.

Once it's done downloading, you'll see the welcome screen and be asked if you want to create a shortcut on your desktop. Tap Start when you are ready.

Once you tap Next, you'll get to the main Samsung Kids UI. It looks a little like your tablet...only cuter! There's a handful of icons on the screen, but you'll notice they each have download buttons. That's because they aren't installed yet. You have to tap the download button for each app you want to install (not more than three at a time).

Swipe to your left, and you'll see non-Samsung apps. These need to be downloaded as well.

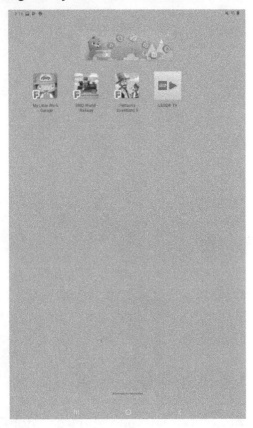

You might be thinking, how safe can this mode be? There's an Internet browser right on the Home screen! Tap it and let's see!

You'll notice right away that this is not yo mama's Internet! The only websites they can access are the ones you add. Want to add one? Tap the +New website button.

You'll quickly notice that all the apps in this mode are very stripped down. Even the camera app, which is pretty harmless, has few features. There's a shutter, a toggle for photos and videos, and a button for effects.

The tablet is the same way. Your child can't open the app and call anyone. They can only call numbers that you've added. Want to add someone? Just tap the + icon.

The pre-installed apps are all pretty harmless, and borderline educational.

If there's apps you want to remove or install, then tap the option button in the upper right corner.

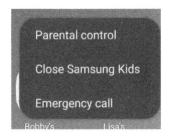

Once you put in your pin, you'll have access to the settings. Here you'll be able to control what your child does and how long they do it for. You can also monitor what they've been doing. You can control how much time they can spend on something like games and something like reading.

Is there a pre-installed app that you don't want your child to see? No problem! Scroll down a little and tap the Apps option.

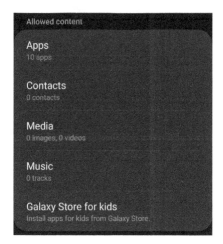

From the options button, select Remove and then select the app that you want removed.

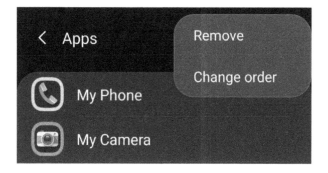

What about other apps? Like third-party ones? Return to that list and select Galaxy Store for kids. That's going to take you to a custom kids' store. It's not going to have teen or adult games—it's only games that are appropriate for kids.

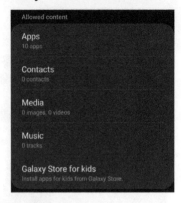

Tap the download option next to any app that you want to download. They'll show up when you swipe right from kids Home screen.

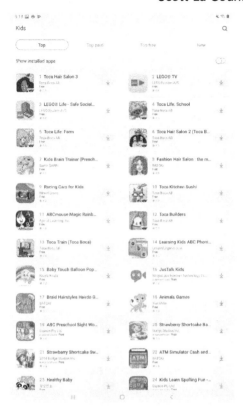

So that's all well and good, but what happens when you want to return to adulthood? How do you get out of this mode? It takes just a second! On the Home screen, tap the back icon. It will ask you for your pin code. Once you add it, you are back in normal mode. That's it!

[6]

SURING THE WEB!

This chapter will cover:
- Setting up email
- Creating and sending email
- Managing multiple accounts
- Browsing the Internet

When it comes to the Internet, there are two things you'll want to do:
- Send email
- Browse the Internet

ADD AN EMAIL ACCOUNT

When you set up your tablet, you'll set it up to your Google Account, which is usually your email.

You may, however, want to add another email account—or remove the one you set up.

To add an email, swipe up to bring up your apps, and tap on Settings.

Next, tap on Accounts.

From here, select Add Account; you can also tap on the account that's been set up and tap re-move account—but remember you can have more than one account on your tablet.

Once you add your email, you'll be asked what type of email it is. Follow the steps after you select the email type to add in your email, password, and other required fields.

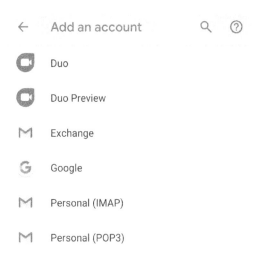

CREATE AND SEND AN EMAIL

To send an email using Gmail (Samsung's native email app), swipe up to get to your apps, tap Gmail, and tap Compose a New Email (the little round, red pencil in the lower right corner). When you're done, tap the Send button.

You can also use the Google Play Store to find other email apps (such as Outlook).

MANAGE MULTIPLE EMAIL ACCOUNTS

If you have more than one Gmail account, tap the three lines at the upper left of your email screen; this brings out a slider menu. If you tap on the little arrow next to the email address, it drops down and will show other accounts. If none are listed, you can add one.

SURFING THE INTERNET

Samsung has an Internet browser. It's pretty good. My advice? Use Google Chrome (also on the tablet). The reason is anywhere else you use the Chrome browser (like your desktop or phone) can be sync-d with the tablet.

Get started by tapping on the Chrome browser icon from your favorite bar, or by going into all programs.

If you've used Chrome on a desktop or any other device, then this chapter won't exactly be rocket science—just like the email app, many of the same properties you find on the desktop exist on the mobile version.

When you open it, you'll see it's a pretty basic browser. There are three main things that you'll want to note.

- **Address Bar** - As you would guess, this is where you put the Internet address you want to go to (google.com, for example); what you should understand, however is that this is not just an address bar. This is a search bar. You can use it to search for things just as you would searching for something on Google; when you hit the enter key, it takes you to the Google search results page.

- **Tab Button** - Because you are limited in space, you don't actually see all your tabs like you would on a normal browser;

instead you get a button that tells you how many tabs are open. If you tap it, you can either toggle between the tabs, or swipe over one of the pages to close the tab.

- **Menu Button** - The last button brings up a menu with a series of other options that I'll talk about next.

→ ☆ ± ⓘ C

New tab

New incognito tab

Bookmarks

Recent tabs

History

Downloads

Share...

Find in page

Add to Home screen

Desktop site ☐

Settings

Help & feedback

The menu is pretty straightforward, but there are a few things worth noting.

"New incognito tab" opens your tablet into private browsing; that doesn't mean your IP isn't tracked. It means your history isn't record; it also means passwords and cookies aren't stored.

A little bit further down is "History"; if you want your history erased so there's no record on your tablet of where you went, then go here and clear your browsing history.

History   ⓘ   🔍   ✕

Your Google Account may have other forms of browsing
history at myactivity.google.com.

CLEAR BROWSING DATA...

If you want to erase more than just websites
(passwords, for example) then go to Settings at the
very bottom of the menu. This opens up more advanced settings.

[7]
TAKING AND MANAGING PICTURES

This chapter will cover:
- How to take different photos
- How to take videos
- Camera settings
- Different camera features

The camera is the bread and butter of the Samsung phone. The tablet? Not so much. Yes, it's there; and yes, it's a pretty good camera. But the idea of trying to hold up a large tablet to take a photo is a little cumbersome for most people.

Still, it's nice to occasionally take photos when you are in a bind.

THE BASICS

Are you ready to get your Ansel Adams on? Let's get started by opening the Camera app

When you open the app, it starts in the basic camera mode. The UI can look pretty simple, but don't be fooled. There are a lot of controls.

In the lower right corner, you'll notice a small, blue icon. The tablet is auto recognizing what setting you are in—night, outdoor, etc. It optimizes the photos appropriately.

If you prefer not to use this, then tap it once and it will no longer be blue. Tap it again to turn it on. It's pretty accurate, but there may still be times when you find it's making your photo look off; if that happens, try turning it off.

On the bottom of the screen is the shutter (to take your photo)—swipe it down to take a "burst shot" which takes several photos at once, and hold it down to toggle to video. To the right of the shutter is the camera flip—to switch to the front camera.

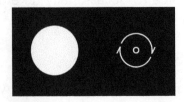

Up on the top of the camera app is where you'll find the majority of your settings.

Starting from left to right, there is the settings icon. Most of the settings are just toggle switches and easy to understand.

Next to that is the flash setting. Tapping that will let you select no flash, auto flash, or force flash.

The next option lets you pick the ration.

One final note on photos (and this applies to videos as well): to zoom, you pinch in and out.

CAMERA MODES

Taking pictures is so yesterday though, isn't it? Tablets are loaded with different modes and Samsung is obviously no stranger to some really great ones.

Think of modes like different lenses. You have your basic camera lens, but then you can also have a lens for fisheye and close up. If you look at the bottom of your camera app, you can slide left and right to get to the different modes.

There are three main ones in the app: photos (which I covered above), videos, and Live Focus (which blurs out the background to give it a more pro look).

Quickly, the video mode has similar features to photo mode.

Up on top, the menu is largely the same as the photo one.

I'll point out two things, however: one, the 9:16 icon will launch the video ratio.

The second thing I'll point out is that little squiggle icon (the last icon you see). This is going to let you draw things as you record.

Just like the other modes, pinching in and out will let you zoom in and out (*but* only for the back camera—the front camera has no zoom).

If you click the More option on the slider, you'll see that there are actually several more photography modes on the tablet. Four more modes to be exact.

If you thought the Photo mode was a little lacking in options and settings, wait until you see the Pro mode!

You can adjust things like ISO, auto focus and more.

Panorama lets you create a panoramic photo; it's great for landscape and cityscape shots.

Food changes settings to give the most ideal focus and effects to take food photos.

Hyperlapse let you capture either slow motion videos or time-lapse videos.

EDITING PHOTOS

Once you take a photo, you can begin fine-tuning it to really make it sparkle. You can access editing by opening the photo you want to make edits to. This is done by either opening it from the camera app by clicking on the photo preview (next to the shutter):

Or by opening the Photo app.

Later in this chapter, I'll write a bit more about how photos are organized, and how you can change things around. For now, we are just talking about editing a photo, so for the purpose of this section, tap on any photo to edit it.

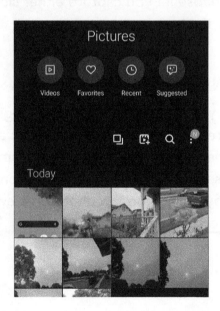

When you open a photo, the options you see will vary depending on what kind of photo you open.

The below example is a Live Focus photo.

As the name suggests, the background is blurred. There's also an option here: Change background effect. This technically isn't editing a photo—when you edit a photo, you go into a different app.

When you tap change the background, you'll have four options. With each option, you can change the intensity of the blur with the slider.

The main blur is simply called "blur"; the next is a spin blur.

The third is a zoom blur.

The last type of blur is color point, which makes the object color and the background black and white.

If you make any changes here, always make sure and tap Apply to save it.

Regardless of the type of photo, there are going to be several options that are the same. Starting on the top, that little play icon will wirelessly show your photo on another device (like a compatible TV).

Next to the play icon is an icon that looks kind of like an eye. That will digitally scan your photo and try and identify what the photo is. In the below example, it finds a flower and gives a link to see more. This feature works pretty well, but isn't always perfect.

Next to the eye icon is an option icon. This will let you set a photo as wallpaper, print it, etc. If you tap Details, it will also let you see when the photo was taken, its resolution, and any tags that have been assigned to it.

On the bottom of any photo are four additional options. The heart icon favorites the photo, the pencil lets you edit it (more on that in a second), the three dots lets you share it, and the trash lets you delete it.

Tap the pencil icon and let's see how to edit a photo next. Regardless of the photo, you'll see the same options on the bottom.

The first option is to crop the photo. To crop, drag the little white corners.

Next is the filter option. The slider lets you select the type of filter, and below that is a slider to adjust the intensity of the filter.

Brightness is the next icon. Each icon here adjusts a different setting (such as the contrast of the photo).

The sticker icon will launch Bitmoji (I'll discuss this later in the chapter), but what this does is let you put stickers on top of your photo.

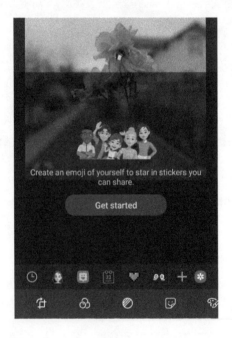

The paintbrush icon lets you draw on top of your photo.

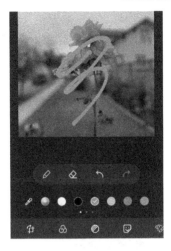

And the text icon lets you write on top of your photo.

If you don't want to spend time editing your photo—you just want it to magically look better with no effort, there's an option up in the upper left corner that will do that for you—it crops, rotates, and adds a filter to it. Depending on how well you took the shot, you may not see much difference.

In the upper right corner is an options menu with even more choices for editing your picture.

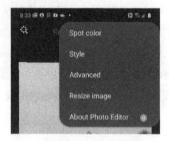

The first is Spot color. Using the little pickers, you can remove a color from the photo to make the subject stand out. To save any changes here, make sure and tap the checkmark; to cancel changes, tap the X.

Style applies filters that give the photo more of an artistic pop—if you want your photo to look like a painting, for example. The slider below it will adjust the intensity.

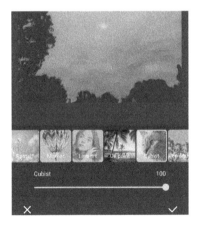

The advanced option will let you do color corrections.

If you took a photo at the highest resolution and are having difficulty sharing it, you can use the Resize image option to make it smaller.

Once you are finished doing edits, make sure and tap Save.

EDITING VIDEOS

Editing a video shares a lot of common features to photos, so make sure and read that section first, as I will not repeat features already referenced above.

To get started open the video that you want to edit, then tap to play it. In the play window, there are going to be a couple of things you should note.

You'll notice the video has the same options at the bottom of it (assuming you haven't played it). To edit it, just tap on that pencil.

The first option you'll see is to crop the video. To crop just drag in or out the white bars before and after the video clip.

Next is the color filter, which works almost identically to the photo filter.

The text icon comes after this and lets you write on top of the photo.

The emoji sticker insert is after this.

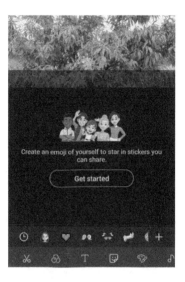

And the paintbrush is second to last.

The last icon is for adding sound. You can add music or anything else you want. You can also use the slider under Video sound to make the videos original sound softer (or nonexistent)—so, for example, you could remove all sound from a family dinner, and replace it with music.

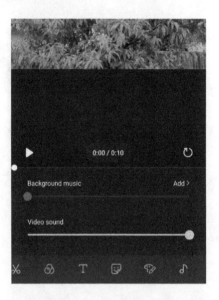

Up on top, there's one option: resolution. If you've recorded in a large format and it's too large, you can use this option to make it smaller.

ORGANIZING YOUR PHOTOS AND VIDEOS

The great thing about mobile photos is you always have a camera ready to capture memorable events; the bad thing about mobile photos is you always have a camera ready to capture events, and you'll find you have hundreds and hundreds of photos very quickly.

Fortunately, Samsung makes it very simple to organize your photos so you can find what you are looking for.

Let's open up the Gallery app and see how to get things organized.

Galaxy keeps things pretty simple by having only four options on the bottom of your screen.

There are four additional options up on top.

In the upper right corner, there's three dots, which is the photo option menu; that menu is there no matter where you are in the Gallery app.

When you tap that menu, you'll get several more options. From this menu you can share an album, create a GIF / collage / Slideshow of the album, or edit the photos / videos in it.

If there's something you are trying to find, tap on the magnifying glass. You can search by what it is (a Live Focus, video, etc.), you can search for tags, you can type an expression (happy photos, for example).

When you tap on Albums, you'll see your albums (Samsung will automatically create some for you), and you can tap on options to create a new album.

Stories lets you capture all your life adventures; you can create a new Story the same way you created an album.

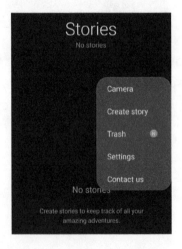

The last option is sharing your photos. To get started, tap the red button

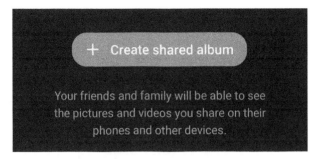

Next, type in a person's tablet number or Samsung ID.

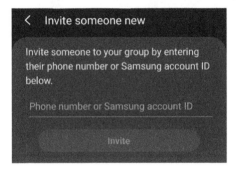

Once you have your shared album created, you can tap the + icon to add photos to it.

You don't have to add all the photos at once. You can continue to add them over time.

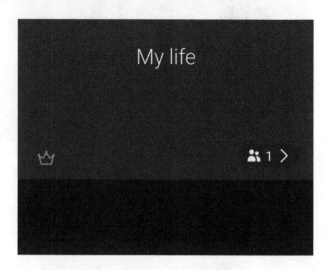

BITMOJI

Bitmoji is the Samsung equivalent of Memoji on the iPhone; it basically lets you create an avatar of yourself that you can use in photos and text messages.

To get started, go to the Camera app, then select More, and finally tap AR Zone.

Next, tap the AR Emoji Camera option.

Before you can have fun, you'll need to take a picture of yourself. Make sure you are in an area with good lighting for the best results.

Once you take the photo, select the gender icon. They are as follows: adult male, adult female, male child, female child. Once you make your selecttion, you'll need wait a few seconds for it to analyze the photo.

Next, you can start using the options to change the way you look and what your avatar is wearing.

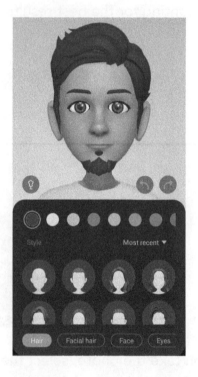

You will now be able to use your AR Camera to take photos with your avatar's head replacing other people's heads!

[8]

BEYOND BASICS

This chapter will cover:
- System settings

If you want to take total control of your Samsung, then you need to know where the system settings are and what can and can't be changed there.

First, the easy part: the system settings are located with the rest of your apps. Swipe up and scroll down to "Settings."

This opens all the settings available:

- Connections
- Sounds and vibrations
- Notifications
- Display
- Wallpaper
- Lock screen
- Biometrics and security
- Privacy
- Location
- Accounts and backup
- Google
- Advanced features
- Digital Wellbeing and parental controls
- Device care
- Apps
- General management
- Accessibility
- Software update
- Tips
- About tablet

I'll cover what each setting does in this chapter. There's a lot of settings! Need to find something quickly? Use the magnifying glass up top. Before looking at the settings, however, tap the avatar of the person in the upper right corner. That's going to let you add in personal information.

CONNECTIONS

This setting, like most settings, does exactly what it sounds like: it manages how things connect to the Internet, Bluetooth, and data usage.

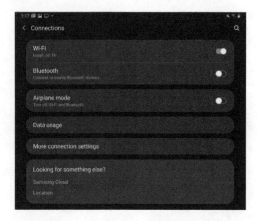

Data usage tells you how much data you've used; tapping on it gives you a deeper overview, so you can see exactly which apps used the data. Why is this important? For most, it probably won't be. I'll give an example of when it helped me: I work on the go a lot; I use the wireless on my tablet to connect my laptop (which is called tethering); my MacBook was set to back up to the cloud, and little did I know it was doing this while connecting to my tablet...20GB later, I was able to pinpoint what happened by looking at the data.

Airplane mode is next. This setting turns off all wireless activity with a switch. So if you're flying and they tell you to turn everything wireless off, you can do it with a switch.

Finally, More connection settings is for doing some wireless connecting on a private network. This is not something a beginning user would need to do, and I'm not going to cover it, as the point of this book is to keep it ridiculously simple. You can also set up wireless printing and wireless emergency alerts here.

SOUNDS AND VIBRATIONS

There's a volume button on the side of your tablet, so why would you need to open up a setting for it?! This setting lets you get more specific about your volume.

For example, you may want your alarm to ring super loud in the morning, but you want your music to play very low.

You can also use these settings to adjust the intensity of vibrations.

NOTIFICATIONS

Notifications are those pop-ups that give you alerts—like new text messages or emails. In the notification setting you can turn them off for some apps while leaving them on for others. You can also enable Do not disturb mode, which will silence all notifications.

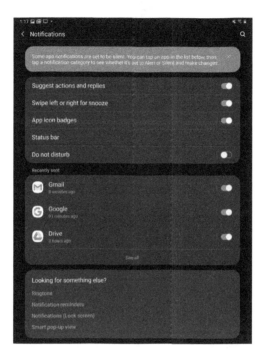

DISPLAY

As with many of the settings, almost all the main features of the Display setting can be changed outside of the app (in the notifications drop-down, for example).

This is where you'll be able to toggle on dark mode, adjust the brightness, turn on adaptive brightness, and toggle blue light on and off.

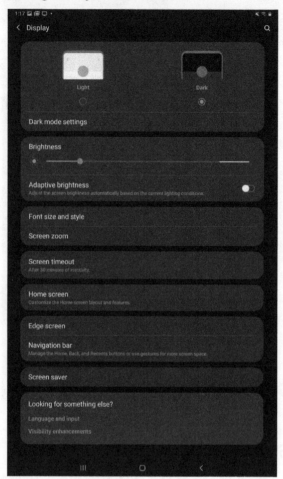

WALLPAPER / THEMES

I'm bundling these two settings together because we've talked about each of them in the section on changing your theme and wallpaper. There are no extra settings here.

LOCK SCREEN

When your tablet is on standby and you lift it up: that's your lock screen. It's the screen you see before you unlock it and get to your Home screen.

The settings here change what shows up there; you can also adjust your lock setting—if, for example, you have a Face ID and want to change it to a pin ID.

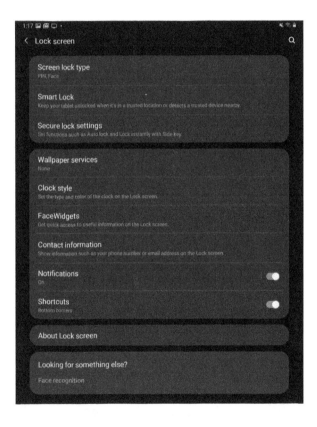

BIOMETRICS AND SECURITY

If you want to add a fingerprint or an additional person to Face ID, you can do so in this menu. You can also update your own—if you didn't do it with glasses, for example, then go here to redo it. You can also toggle on Find My Mobile, which lets you trace where your tablet is if you've misplaced it or left it behind.

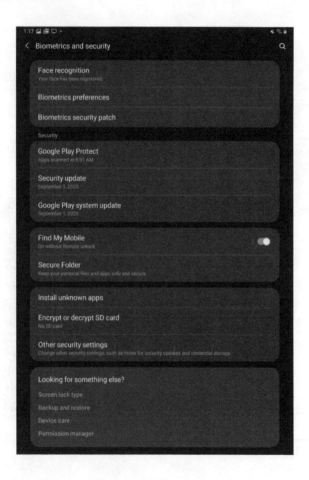

PRIVACY

Like Location Control (covered below), Privacy settings got a big upgrade in Android 10. It's so big, it now fills an entire section in the settings.

The biggest upgrade is the ability to customize what apps see what; it's no longer all or nothing. You can refine exactly how much or how little each app can see.

Tap on Permissions as one example of what you can control.

LOCATION

In the past, Location Control was an all or nothing feature—you'd decide if an app could see you all the time or none of the time. That's nice for privacy, but not nice for when you actually need someone to know your location—like when you are getting picked up by a ride app like Lyft. The new Android OS adds a new option for while you are using the app. So, for example, a ride app can only see your location while you are using the app; once the ride is over, they can no longer see what you are doing.

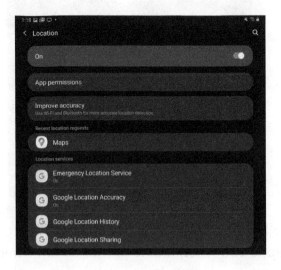

ACCOUNTS & BACKUP

If you have more than one Google account, you can tap on this to add it. If you want to remove your current account, tap on it and tap Remove—

remember, however, you can have more than one account. Don't remove it just so you can add another.

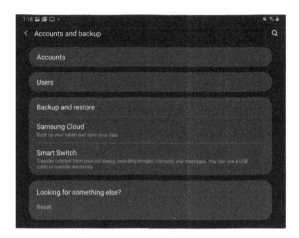

You can also come here to back up your tablet. It's good to do it once a month or so, but you definitely want to do it before switching to a new device.

GOOGLE

Google is where you will go to manage any Google device connected with your tablet. If you are using a Google watch, for example, or a Chromecast.

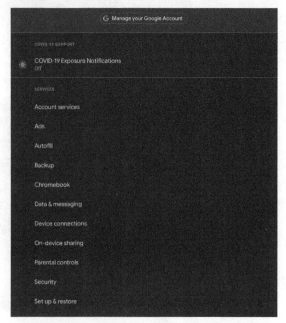

ADVANCED FEATURES

Most the features in Advanced Features are exactly what they sound: Advanced. They're features that novice users will likely never use. Things like screenshot recording features and reducing animations.

There's one important one here. One I recommend everyone use: Side key.

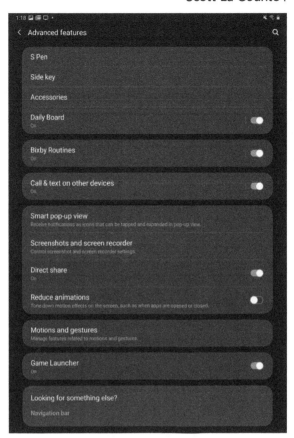

Side key is that button below the volume. Right now, if you hold it down, it goes to Bixby. Bixby isn't Samsung's most popular feature. Some people like it—many don't. If you want to change that button to power down your tablet instead, then click that.

When you double tap the button, it launches the camera. You can update that too.

DIGITAL WELLBEING AND PARENTAL CONTROLS

Digital Wellbeing is my least favorite feature on the Samsung tablet; now when my wife says, "You spend too much time on your tablet"—she can actually prove it! The purpose of the setting is to help you manage your time more. It lets you know you're spending 12 hours a day updating your social media with memes of cats, and "hopefully" make you feel like perhaps you shouldn't do that.

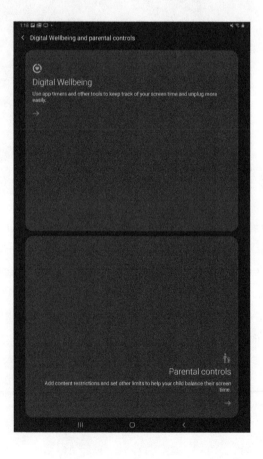

If you have kids using your tablet, this is where you can also set up parental controls.

DEVICE CARE

Samsung tries to make it simple to take care of your tablet. With one click (the blue Optimize now), you can have your tablet scanned and any problematic apps will be closed.

You can also tap on any of the three sections: Battery, Storage, and Memory.

The battery setting is more about analytics than settings you can change. There are some settings here you can edit—you can put your tablet in battery saving mode, for example. This setting is more useful if your battery is draining too quickly; it helps you troubleshoot what's going on so you can get more life from your tablet.

When you first get your tablet, storage won't be a big issue, but once you start taking photos (which are larger than you think) and installing apps, it's going to go very quickly.

The storage setting helps you manage this. It shows you what's taking up storage, so you can decide if you want to delete things. Just tap on any of the subsections and follow the instructions for what to do to save space.

APPS

Every app you download has different settings and permissions. A map app, for example, needs your permission to know your location. You can turn these permissions on and off here. Does it really matter? App makers can't abuse it, right? Sort of. Here's an example: a few months ago, a popular ride-sharing app made headlines because it wanted to know where passengers were after they left the ride, so they could promote different restaurants and stores and make even more money. Many felt this was both greedy and an invasion of privacy; if you are of the latter stance, then you could go in here and stop sharing your location.

How? Just tap Advanced then look at all the permissions you are giving away. Go to the permission you are concerned with and toggle the app from on to off.

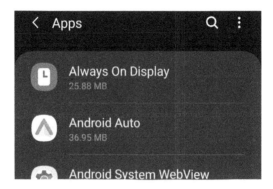

GENERAL MANAGEMENT

General management is where you go to change the language and date / time; the most important thing here, however, is Reset. This is where you can do a complete factory reset of your tablet.

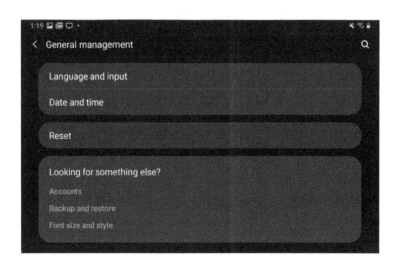

ACCESSIBILITY

Do you hate tablets because the text is too small, the colors are all wrong, you can't hear anything? Or something else? That's where accessibility can help. This is where you make changes to the device to make it easier on your eyes or ears.

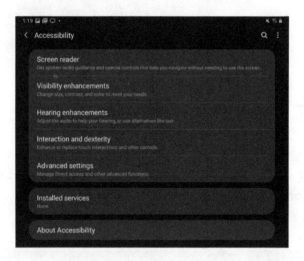

Let's dig in a little more what you will find in each of the menus.

SCREEN READER

Screen reader reads back whatever is on your phone. Push a button? It reads what that button says. Tapping the toggle will turn it on.

Clicking on settings will bring up settings for the voice. You can change how fast it speaks, if it speaks passwords and caller ID aloud, and more.

VISIBILITY ENHANCEMENTS

Visibility Enhancements changes the contrasts for people who have difficulty seeing. It also lets you change the shapes of buttons to make them stand out more.

Under Size and Zoom you can turn magnification on and off; this is useful if you want apps to be larger, so you can read things without glasses.

HEARING ENHANCEMENTS

Hearing enhancements is where you go to make things amplified, change to mono audio, and add hearing aid support. You can also turn on Real Time Text and Live Captioning so you can read what you might not otherwise be able to hear.

At the bottom of settings is Sound detectors, which lets you get notifications on your phone when it detects that someone has rang your door-bell or there's a baby crying.

INTERACTION AND DEXTERITY

If you find that when you tap, things don't open, then Interaction and Dexterity is a setting that can help adjust the sensitivity of touch, which may make it more responsive.

ADVANCED SETTINGS

The advance menu lets you turn your volume up / down and side button into shortcut keys. For example, you can set volume up to open an app instead of turn the volume up. You can also set up flash notifications, so your flash goes off anytime that you get an alert.

SOFTWARE UPDATE

This is where you will find general information about your tablet, such as the OS you are running, the kind of tablet you have, IP address, etc. It's more of an FYI, but there are a few settings here that you can change.

TIPS & SUPPORT

This isn't really a setting. It's just tips and support. You can also talk with support here.

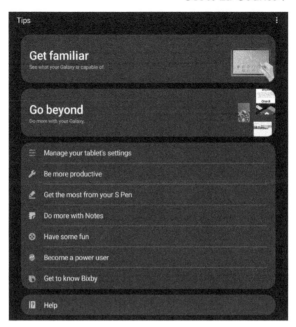

ABOUT TABLET

This is where you will find general information about your tablet. Such as the OS you are running, the kind of tablet you have, IP address, etc. It's more of an FYI, but there are a few settings here that you can change.

BONUS BOOK: GOOGLE DOCS

Disclaimer: Please note, while every effort has been made to ensure accuracy, this book is not endorsed by Alphabet, Inc. and should be considered unofficial.

INTRODUCTION

Like hundreds of millions of people, you probably lived your whole life using one-word processing tool: Microsoft Word.

It's great software! Powerful software! Resourceful software! And...expensive software!

Google Docs is the Google equivalent of Microsoft Word, but it's free. Free as in ad-supported, right? One paragraph in and you have to watch a 30 second video of some emoji game you would never play! Wrong! Free as in free. As in no ads. Nothing to pay later. Free!

Who wouldn't want software like that? For the price of nothing you are getting something you used to pay for. And that nothing doesn't get you second-rate software that doesn't help you do the things you really want to do. It gets you cloud-based software that is on par with all the other word processing tools out there.

In many ways, it's actually better then other tools.

If you are interesting in learning more about it, or you are ready to make the leap and become a free user, then this guide will show you the ropes and get you started as quick as possible.

Let's get started!

THE GOOGLE DRIVE CRASH COURSE

This chapter will cover:
- Why is it free?
- Creating files
- Finding files

GOOGLE DRIVE

Before talking about the star of this book (Google Docs), it's worth spending a little bit of time with Google Drive.

Google Drive is the where all your beautiful Docs will be stored.

GOOGLE DRIVE OVERVIEW

Every computer has "local" storage, which is where all the stuff (files, photos, documents), is stored directly on the computer. Windows computers have File/System Explorer, Mac Computers have Finder, and Google has Google Drive—it's the same concept you are accustomed to on your home computer, but it's all online.

Google Drive is basically an online version of a file directory; whatever you create in Google is stored here—think of it like Google's version of DropBox. In fact, you can also store files here—photos, videos, PDFs—whatever you want.

To get started, go to drive.google.com. If you are not signed in to a Google account, then you'll be greeted by a lovely screen that looks a little like the one below:

Click that "Go to Google Drive" blue button and you'll see an option that looks like the below:

While Google Docs is free to use, you do need a Google account to use it. So that's the catch, right? Free to use, but you have to pay to get a Google account? Nope! A Google account is also free. If you use Gmail, then you already have one, and can use that to sign in.

Once you are all signed in you'll see the main interface. The side pane is your main navigation. This is where you will see all of your folders. It's probably empty right now, unless you've started using it.

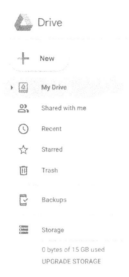

Two things to note here:

1. Shared with me—if people share documents or folders with you, they'll be here unless you move them.
2. Starred—to help you stay organized, you can "star" documents. When you "star" them, they will still be in your main directory, but they'll be here as well.

If you have the basic free plan, you'll have 15 GBs of storage. That's obviously a lot. Considering that a document is very small, you'll probably never want more—unless you are also using Google Drive to store videos and files, or to back up your entire computer.

Why on Earth would you want to pay to back up your computer on the cloud? Because it's surprising cheap! The rates below are what you can expect—they might go up after this book is printed, but not by much since they've been this low for a while.

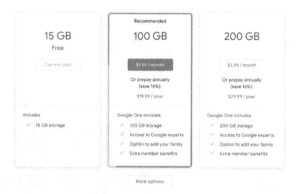

Most people have around 200 GBs of data floating around. That means, for less than a dinner for two at Olive Garden, you can safely know that your data is protected online!

Why back it up online? Two reasons:

1. What if your house floods or burns down and you don't have time to get your computer. Think of all the memories you would lose that are stored on your computer.

2. What if you are away on business or a family trip and you really need a document. It's safely online and you can access it anytime.

If you want to back up your entire computer to Google Drive, you just need to download some software that will sync your computer to the cloud. That means if you save a new file, that file automatically goes to the cloud and you don't have to do a thing. You can also pick and choose what folders are synced to the cloud. To get the software, go to the address below:

https://support.google.com/drive/answer/2424368?co=GENIE.Platform%3DDesktDD&hl=en

CREATING FILES AND DOCS

Once you're ready to create either a document (such as a doc, spreadsheet or presentation), click the new button in the left menu pane:

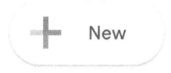

This will bring up several choices. The main three apps are on the bottom of this menu, but if you click "more" you can see some of the useful, but lesser used, Google Apps (I'm looking at you Google Jamboard!). You can also access this menu by right- clicking inside Google Drive:

🗁	Folder	
🗋	File upload	
🗀	Folder upload	
📄	Google Docs	>
📊	Google Sheets	>
🖼	Google Slides	>
	More	>

This is also where you'll go to upload files from your computer, or to create a new folder.

Creating folders will help you stay organized. You may, for example, have a recipe folder, or school folder, or a bills folder—you can have as many folders as you want. You can also create folders inside folders (and folders inside the folder you just created inside the folder—go ahead and figure that sentence out...I'll wait!). It's just like file organization on your computer.

If you want to create a folder within a folder, you can either open that folder up and select the new button, or you can right-click inside that open folder and select "Folder."

STARRING AND SHARING FILES

Once the docs are created, you'll be able to right-click them at any time to bring up a new menu that's just for that specific file. You can add a star to it, rename it, preview it, and, of course, share it.

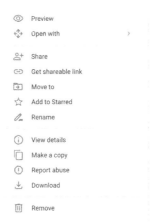

Once you click "Get sharable link" (the option for sharing a file with other people), you'll see something a little like this:

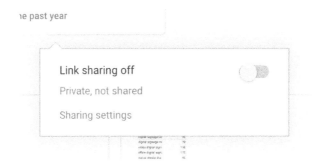

If it's white, like the above, it will note that sharing is off. To turn it on, just click that white box, and it will turn green and note that sharing is turned on. It will also give you a link to the document.

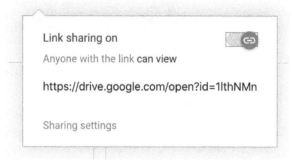

When it's on, by default, it's a non-public link. That means the only way someone is going to find it is if you give them the link.

If you click "Sharing settings" you'll get a few more options. You can email a person the link and also make them an editor, or give them all access.

Click the "Anyone with the link can view" drop down and you can manage the access, for example, if you only want certain people that you email to see it—note: if you select this option, they will need to be signed into a Google Account (the one you used in the email name in the box under this), to see the doc.

If you select "More" you'll have a few more options. One is to make the file public. This means it's going to be searchable to anyone on Google and people may find it randomly—people you don't know—so it's best if you don't make your Google Sheet with the names and phone numbers of "People with excessive gas" public.

FIND FILES

Files are pretty easy to find when you are first getting started. But they add up quickly—especially if you are using them for school or business, or if you are backing up all the files on your computer.

Fortunately, Google has a search bar that works remarkably well—it's right on top of Google Drive. You don't have to know the name of the file—you can search for what's in the document. So if you can't remember what you named your Google Doc, but you know it had the line "And that is why I love competitive dog grooming" (yes, it's a thing!), then just type in that phrase and it will find your doc.

Q Search Drive

If it's returning too many results—because you have obviously written countless scholarly papers on the subject of competitive dog grooming—then click that little arrow next to the search bar.

That brings up an advanced search. You'll be able to search by owner, by those that are starred, when it was lasted opened, what kind of file it is, and more. Once you've added in all your filters, just hit search, and it will return results in seconds.

GOOGLE DOCS CRASH COURSE

This chapter will cover:
- Why use Word?
- The Crash Course
- Accessibility settings
- Getting Started

WHY IS IT FREE?

You are probably wondering "If it's so great then why is it free?" You don't give away great software for free, right? There has to be a catch! There's always a catch! Are they taking your data and selling it on the black market? First, no! Second, not everyone is out to get you, so just simmer down!

The Google you know gives all their tools away. How exactly do they make money? Does some rich guy donate a penny every time someone Googles "cute cat photos"? Definitely not—no one is that wealthy! Google makes money by selling ads, cloud services, selling apps, and a number of other things which all adds up to billions of dollars.

So there are ads in Google Docs? Nope! It all goes back to Google's business model. Unlike Microsoft, who is trying to make money off its software, Google is trying to make money off its service. It wants schools and businesses to use its enterprise services.

The Google Docs that we use is free; but for businesses that want to add dozens of workers, or schools who want to add hundreds of students, there is a charge.

If you are a small business, then there's a good chance you could probably make do with the free version. Plus, if Google is managing your company's email account, then you are paying for the service already.

SHOULD I THROW AWAY WORD AND NEVER LOOK BACK?

Before getting started, let's talk about the elephant in the room: Microsoft Word!

Does Google Docs make Word irrelevant? It really depends on the user. For most people, Google Docs can probably accomplish what you want to do.

Microsoft is paid software, but it's also a lot more powerful. If you are running macros, or doing mail mergers, and need other advanced features, then you'll probably want to stick with Word. There are add-ons for Google Docs, but they just don't beat what you'll find in the full version of Microsoft Word.

If you are just doing basic writing, then Google Docs will be just fine. When it comes to collaboration, it's more than just fine; while Microsoft has made great strides towards making it easier to share and collaborate in Word, Google is the one who mastered the idea. Google also has plug-ins for editing tools such as Grammarly, and is making a big push to be more responsive to catching basic grammatical errors.

Personally, I use Google Docs almost daily, but I still have a copy of Word on my desktop, and that's what I use for my final draft. Once collaboration is finished, I copy and paste it into Word and apply all the final touches.

THE CRASH COURSE

Before we jump into creating our first document, I'll go over the main Google Docs toolbar. If you've ever used Word, then you'll probably know what most of these do already. If you ever get stuck, then hover over the icon and it will give you a description of what it does.

The first two icons are your undo, redo icons. This undoes or redoes whatever you just typed:

Next is the Print, spellcheck, and formatter. You probably know what the first two are. The last one is a handy little tool; it copies the format of the text. So let's say I have text that is bold, 14- point in size. I can highlight that text, select the paint roller, then click on the text I want to apply the style to. Instantly that text is changed to the same style.

The 100% is the zoom. If you want to zoom out to see more (but smaller) text on the screen, then click on that:

Fonts and style is next to that. This is where you can select the style (if it's a Heading, for example), the font family, the font size, and if you want to bold, italicize, underline, or change the color of the text.

The insert options is the next section. These are all the things you may want to insert into a doc. That includes a link, a comment, and an image:

Justification is next to that. If you want to right align, center align, or change the line spacing, you'll use these options:

If you want to create a numbered or bulleted list, you can use the next two icons; next to those are the indentation:

If you have formatting you want to reset, you can use the icon below. This is good if you've copied text from the web and you want to reset it to the default Google Docs text size:

The last two options change how you are viewing a document and to hide the toolbar:

That's a high-level overview. These things will make more sense as we go.

LET'S TALK ABOUT ACCESSIBILITY

Perhaps a better subheading here would be "Let's Talk About Accessibility...or the lack thereof." There's not a lot here in the way of accessibility.

Where Google Apps really shines, however, is the openness of the software—it allows developers to add apps into the software; so if you don't see something, then chances are there's an app for that.

Let's start with the basics: there is, in fact, accessibility. Go the top menu, then tools, and Accessbility Features (near the bottom)

This brings up a popup with all the Accessibility settings available. There's only one "Turn on screen reader support." If you want that, then check it off.

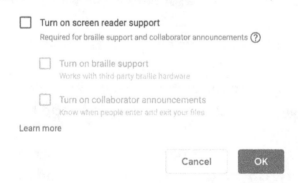

The most common thing people want to do is just make the text bigger so you can read it easier. You could change the font size for that, but the more practical solution is just to change the zoom size. Go to the menu toolbar where it says "100%."

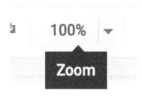

Now just change it to a larger number.

Something else that is helpful is text-to-speech. That means you can read back allowed what's on the screen. Unfortunately, that is not a native feature to Google Apps, but like I said before, if you don't see it, then chances are a developer has made it. In the case of text-to-speech, there are several. Go to the top menu, select "Add-ons" next to help, and click "Get add-ons."

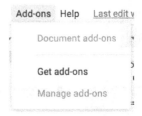

From here, search for what you want—text-to speech in this example. Then follow the instructions to install it.

Personally, I don't use an add on. I use a Chrome browser plugin from TTSReader.com. The way this app works is anytime you want something read back, you click the button in your browser, and paste it in. I like it because it's not tied to any one software or tool. There's a free version that's add supported, or a premium version that's $9.99. There are dozens and dozens just like this app, so I encourage you to do your homework and find the best one for you.

One last thing I will note here is that every browser has accessibility settings. Because Google Apps is browser based, there's browser features that might help you as well. As you look into accessibility, don't forget to look up what settings your preferred Internet browser supports.

GETTING STARTED

Okay, so how exactly do you use Google Docs? There are several ways, but the quickest is to just type in drive.google.com.

Once you have your Google account, then you are all set. Repeat the step above and the browser Window should look more like the below:

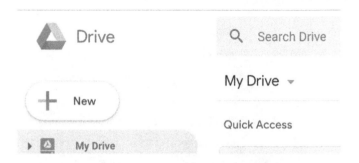

Docs really shines through its connection to Google Drive. Anything you start in Google Docs is automatically saved in your Google Drive account—no need to worry about losing work through power failures, device catastrophes, or really just about any other scenario. Changes are saved as you go, and so are the various versions of your document, so it's easy to revert to an earlier stage of a draft if you need to.

YOUR FIRST DOCUMENT

This chapter will cover:
- Creating your first document
- Titling your Google Doc
- Opening saved docs

CREATING YOUR FIRST DOC

Now that you have your account, let's create a document. Click on the "New" button and then hover over Google Docs; there are two options: Black document and From a template. For now, select "From a template." I'll cover templates a little bit later.

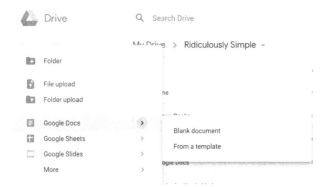

This is going to open up a new tab, and your Google Docs editor will appear.

If you're a Word or Pages user, then you'll be relieved to know everything is designed to work the same way. Many of the buttons look identical.

So, you don't need this book, right?! There's still a difference, and that's what we'll spend the most time with in this book.

Let's have some fun. Pretend the American Revolution is taking place in the year 2019 instead of the year 1776. The British have put fines on our beloved Internet usage, and the people have had enough! Why should you have to pay to see videos of adorable puppies on skateboards?

Michelle Obama is the leader of the American colonies. She's been working on the first draft of a proclamation with her first man, Barack Obama.

The first thing she needs is a title.

HOW TO TITLE YOUR GOOGLE DOC

Look up in the upper left-hand corner of your Google Docs editor. See the text field that says, "Untitled Document." That's every Google Docs default title. Click on it.

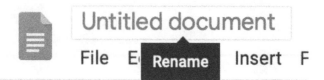

You can now add any title you want by typing. I'll pick something highly original: "The Declaration of Independence," but you can pick anything you want. When you finish, hit the enter key.

In a flash, watch that top bar change with your new title. As long as it shows the new title, then it worked.

Need even more assurance? Look to the right of it: it should say "All changes saved"? Guess what?! It saved!

All changes saved in Drive

It may not seem all that revolutionary today, but everything saves automatically. You don't need to hit CTRL S every few seconds. Google saves as you type. If you are the paranoid type, then you still can save manually.

Let's start things off by creating a headline for our doc. Let's go crazy and use Corsiva, 18-point font. You only live once, right?

This hopefully feels familiar to you—it's essentially the same way you do it in other document editors. I bet you've used this type of toolbar hundreds of times before. Here's the take away here: icons that look like they do in another app tend to do the exact same thing they did in that other app.

My Glorious Heading!

So let's write the title and first paragraph of our declaration, then in a moment we'll send it off for review.

Everything is looking good so far, right? But what happens if there's a power outage? In a blink of a second, it all goes dark. How do we get back to where we left off?

OPENING A SAVED DOCUMENT

Close your browser. Make sure Google Docs has completely gone away.

Now go right back to drive.google.com.

Unless you are on a public computer (like at a library), Google will show you all the files you have created. Since it was the last thing you worked on, you should see The Declaration of Independence right at the top in the Quick Access list.

Quick Access

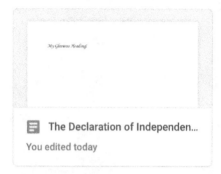

If you are just getting started, it will also be the only doc you see, and you can access it below the quick access; it will look a "little" like this:

The Declaration of Independence   me   7:16 AM

I say "little" because you might be in list view or you might be in grid view. What's the difference? List view looks like the above—it gives the name, who the owner is, and the time it was edited. Grid view is more of a thumbnail preview of the doc, like this:

The Declaration of Independ...

Notice how author and time lasted edited is gone?

What's better? It's a preference, but if you are working with dozens of documents, then Grid view probably will not be ideal unless you need to see previews.

To toggle between the two, click these icons in the upper corner:

List is the horizontal lines, and grid is the six square boxes.

The top spot goes to documents that have been recently edited.

When you double-click on "The Declaration of Independence," it opens up in a new tab. It's basically the same as opening a document back up in Word—the difference: It's in the cloud.

You can also right-click it to see more options—one of them is "Open with" and you can open it by clicking Google Docs.

This option would be useful if you have a Chromebook that has other editing tools installed and you don't want to use Google Docs to edit it. For it to work, however, you need to have those other apps installed.

You can do that by going to the Chrome extensions store:

https://chrome.google.com/webstore/category/extensions

This is a marketplace for all things Chrome, and most of the extensions (or apps) are free. Just make sure you are using Chrome—hence the name. If you aren't, you can still see the page, but you'll be greeted with this subtle notice:

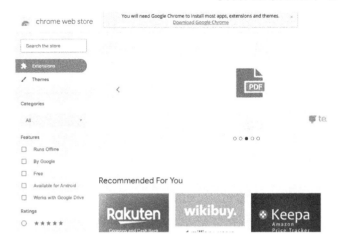

Like most Word Processing editors today, if you open it on a different device (i.e. smartphone or tablet), it's going to look pretty similar. Anything you change on those devices will reflect the document everywhere. It's all in the cloud.

Users of mobile devices (such as iPhones and iPads) can see Google Docs will need a native app to make edits, but what I'm talking about in this book is essentially identical on the apps.

Unfortunately, you'll need a separate app for every app you are using. So you need to get the Google Drive app and the Google Docs app—and if you plan on using Google Slides or Sheets, you'll need to get those apps too. Fortunately, they're free.

Your device has an app store, and that's where you'll download them—just type in the name of the app. The exception here is Fire tablets; these tablets have a not-so-nice relationship with Google that I won't go into here. Google won't put their apps in the app store because of that not-so-nice relationship. You can still install them, but you would need to do something called "side load app." That basically means you are downloading the app onto an SD card, putting the card into the tablet, and installing it manually. I'm not covering how to do that in this book, but if installing it on a Fire device is a must, then there are plenty of tutorials for that. Do so at your own risk, as it's not exactly supported by the device.

SHARING IS CARING

This chapter will cover:
- How to share docs
- Editing and collaborating

HOW TO SHARE YOUR GOOGLE DOCS

Google Docs is hands-down one of the easiest ways to work on a group document.

When two or more people are editing a document at the same time, you'll be able to see that person's cursor position and watch edits in real time. If you're concerned about losing work, remember that Google Docs saves the version history for you, so it's easy to revert if you need to. Click File > See revision history (or press CTRL+ALT+SHIFT+G). By default, revisions are shown grouped into daily periods, but if you want to see changes made by the minute, click "Show more detailed revisions" at the bottom of the revisions panel. You can see which collaborator made each change in a group document. Of course, the slightly less elegant Undo and Redo functions are always available as well!

Back to your masterpiece in progress: The Declaration of Independence. Michelle is ready for a second opinion of what she's done.

She knows Barack is a master orator, so she knows he's going to have some good input.

Look up in the upper right corner. See the blue button that says Share? Click on that. It's going to open up several different sharing options.

There's a few ways to share it:
1. Type their email address and let Google do the rest.
2. Manually (covered below).

When you email someone, you can also manage exactly what they can do. Click that little pencil icon. By default, it will say they can edit the doc. You can change it so they can only comment on the doc, or they can only view the doc:

You can also hit advance at the bottom of the share menu, and have a few more features—such as disabling print:

But let's say you don't want to email the first man. Let's say you just want to give him a link— that way he doesn't need to use his Google account to open it. To do that, follow the steps above, but in the upper corner of the box, click "Get shareable link."

Once you click that, it will give you a sharable link—it even copies the link so if you hit CTRL-V (or right-click paste) you can paste that link anywhere you want.

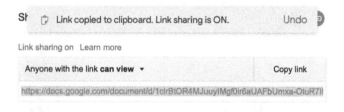

If you click on can view, it will give you a drop-down menu with more features. It looks sort of like the other drop-down menu above, but there's an option that says "more."

When you click on "More," it gives you a few extra features—such as making the document public in search engines so anyone can find it.

Link sharing

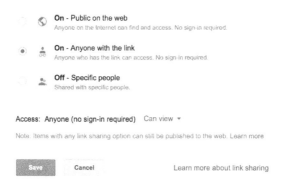

Access: Anyone (no sign-in required)   Can view ▾

Note. Items with any link sharing option can still be published to the web. Learn more

Save   Cancel   Learn more about link sharing

You can turn sharing off at any time, by hitting the "Share" button; once it's turned off, anyone who goes to that link—even if they've been there before—won't be able to see it. If you've emailed a person, they are still a viewer until you remove them.

If you have a person who really hates Google Docs and refuses to view your document in anything but Word, Google Docs allows you to export your work to a Word Document so you don't have to do all of the copying and font processing yourself. Just click on file > download as > Word; there's a whole host of other exports here as well.

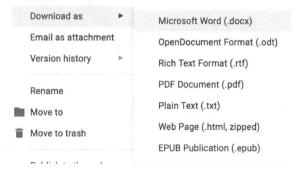

EDITING AND COLLABORATING WITH OTHERS

Let's pretend for a moment the first man is in the document and he's ready to make some changes and add some notes.

As he goes through the document, he's going to make some notes. There are a few ways to do it; the easiest way is to right-click and select "Comment."

You can also get this, by selecting Insert on the toolbar, and Comment:

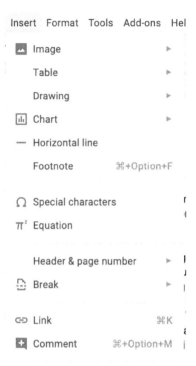

Either of these will bring up the comment box. Add your comment, and select the blue comment box when you are ready to post it. When you add a comment (or make a change), it's in real-time; that means if the person who is collaborating with you has the document open, they can actually watch you make the edits and add the comments.

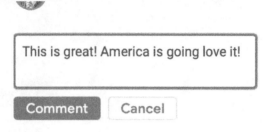

If you have multiple people working on the doc, you can type "@" and see a list of people you can mention; if you mention them, Google will notify them so they can add a reply to your comment.

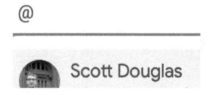

Once the comment is posted, it will show up on the side of Google Docs.

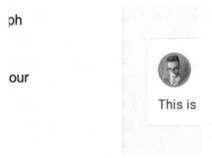

You can delete or edit the comment by clicking on those three little dots on the side of the box:

The person on the other end will be able to resolve the comment (that makes it disappear, but they can undo it).

Or they can reply to it.

When others are editing a doc I created, my personal preference is to tell them to edit with suggestions. This lets me see the changes they have made. You can turn it on by clicking on the pencil icon in the menu, and selecting "Suggesting."

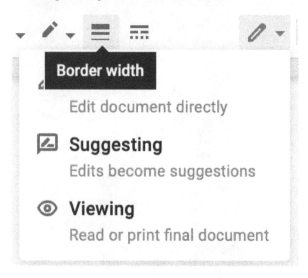

Now when they edit the doc, it will show up as a different color.

This is a test

If you click on what they changed, you can accept the change with the check mark, or ignore it with the X. You can also ask questions about it and they can reply.

To see all the versions of a document, go to "file" and see versions.

If there is going to be a lot of versions, then one suggestion is to name each one—which you can do here.

When you click "See version history", you'll get a list of all the versions. Clicking on any one of them will bring up that version. You can view it, or even restore it.

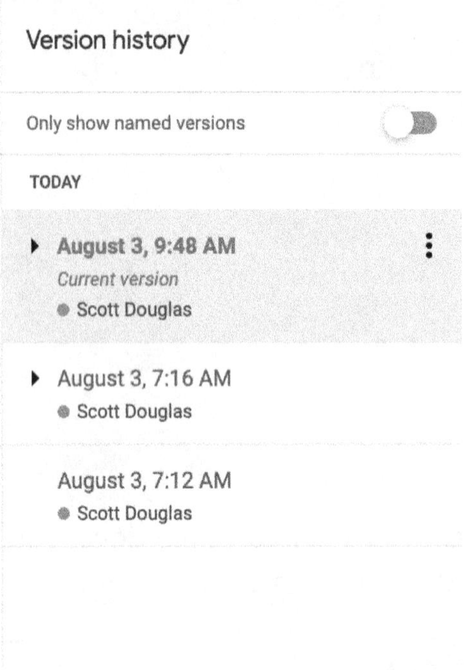

Version history

Only show named versions

TODAY

▸ **August 3, 9:48 AM**
Current version
● Scott Douglas

▸ August 3, 7:16 AM
● Scott Douglas

August 3, 7:12 AM
● Scott Douglas

To get back to the document, just hit the back button in the menu (not the browser back button):

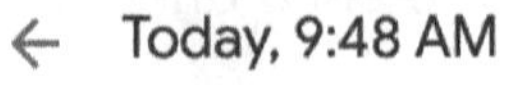

← Today, 9:48 AM

BEYOND THE BASICS

This chapter will cover:
- Printing
- Adding photos
- Adding tables
- Adding spreadsheets
- Adding a table of contents
- Templates

PRINTING FROM THE CLOUD

Michelle's pretty happy with her declaration, but she's still a little old school—she likes to read through her work the old fashion way with that little thing called paper. So, she obviously needs to print it.

You probably can guess that you do this a way you are familiar with: File > Print.

From here, it gets a little...complicated. Printing is not something Google Docs excels at.

You have two main options:

Save it to your computer and then print it from your computer.

Add your computer to Google

If you want to add your computer to Google Cloud print, then click the link.

Getting Started with Google Cloud Print

Classic printers

Classic Printers connect to a laptop or PC, and register with Google Cloud Print using a feature of Google Chrome. Learn more.

Add Classic printer

Cloud Print printers

Cloud Ready Printers connect directly to the internet and can register themselves with Google Cloud Print without a laptop or PC. Learn more.

Add Cloud Ready printer

It will walk you through the steps. The steps change depending on the kind of printer you have. It's not rocket science, but you'll need to pay attention to details.

If you want to skip the fuss there's a longer, but less hassle, way: export as a PDF, open the PDF on your computer, print it from your computer. Because you already have a printer on your computer, it will show up when you do File > Print.

ADDING PHOTOS TO GOOGLE DOCS

Okay, so you've printed it, you've agreed the text is where you want it to be by collaborating with others—now you want to jazz it up.

Google Docs works just like any other word processor. You can add in images wherever you want, either by copying and pasting, or by adding them in from Insert > Image.

Just find a place where you want to add an image. If you have found the image online and copied it, then just do CTRL-V, and it will be added in.

If you have the image stored on your computer, in your Google Drive, or any number of other places, then you can do one of two things. One: click Insert > Image:

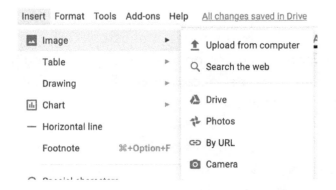

Or, two, click the Picture icon in the toolbar:

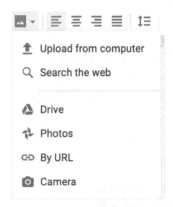

If you simply want to add the image from your computer, then choose "Upload from computer"

and find it on your computer. You can also search the web for the file, paste a link to the file, or, if you are using a device that supports it, use the computer's built-in camera to add an image.

Once the image is in your document, click on it. You'll see little blue squares around it—and a small blue dot:

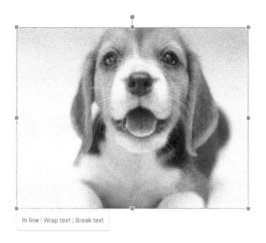

In line | Wrap text | Break text

Clicking on these lets you resize the image; clicking on the dot will let you rotate the image. You can also choose how the text communicates with the image. By default, it will be Inline—that means the text will go above and below it. "Wrap text" will mean the text will go on all sides of it. "Break text" lets you put a margin around the text—if you want a little white space, for example.

If you right-click, you'll also see some extra options for the image:

Most options you probably understand. "Alt text" is handy if you'll be publishing this online—it is text that shows if the text can't be seen; you are basically describing the image.

Clicking on "Image options" will bring up even more options:

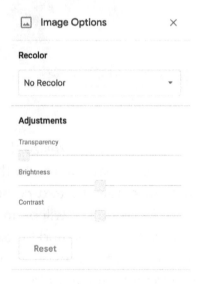

Here you can make it brighter, for example; you can also make it semi-transparent—which is great if you will be using it as a watermark.

If you change your mind about the image, you can delete it or you can just click "Replace image" when you click on it:

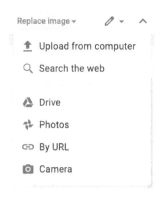

GETTING REALLY FANCY

We have photos. It's looking snazzy, right?! Now let's dig in deeper.

Next, we are going to learn how to add in tables and spreadsheets. This might not be for everyone, but it's still good to know.

First, let's see how to do this the manual way. This is a good option if you don't have a lot of data you are working with—let's pretend here that you want to show the week's lunch menu.

Go to "Insert" on the toolbar and "Table":

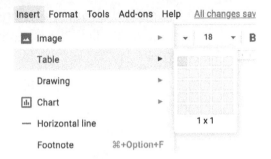

From here, you'll drag the number of boxes based on how big you want your table to be. This is a lunch menu, and I'm going to make it seven days with two rows.

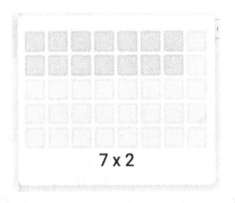

It will show up blank:

Next, I'll add in my menu. I'm personally excited for Saturday, where lunch will be a bag of Doritos—I really put a lot of effort into that lunch!

Sunday	Monday	Tuesday	Wednesday	Thursday	Friday	Saturday
Green eggs and ham	Lobster	Hamburger	Lambchops	Fish & Chips	FREE DAY	Bag of doritos

That table is nice, but it doesn't really visually illustrate anything. Next, I'm going to change the color of the top row so it stands out a bit more. Highlight that entire top row:

Sunday	Monday	Tuesday	Wednesday	Thursday	Friday	Saturday

Next, right-click, which will bring up your "Table" menu. Select "Table properties." This kind of sounds like the properties for the entire table, but because we highlighted and then right-clicked, it will only change the style of the row highlighted (if we had right-clicked without highlighting, it would have changed everything).

Merge cells

Distribute rows
Distribute columns

Table properties

Select all matching text
Update 'Normal text' to match

There's a lot of properties here, but the one we want for this row is "Cell background color":

Once you change the background, click "OK" and the table will look similar to the below:

Sunday	Monday	Tuesday	Wednesday	Thursday	Friday	Saturday
Green eggs and ham	Lobster	Hamburger	Lambchops	Fish & Chips	FREE DAY	Bag of doritos

You can also highlight one row and change the color. I'll change Friday because it's a free day and I want it to stand out more.

Let's pretend we don't want cow meat this week—we want two days of lobster! Delete "hamburger," highlight both the Monday and Tuesday boxes, right-click, and select "merge cells":

The cell is now one box:

Sunday	Monday	Tuesday	Wednesday	Thursday	Friday	Saturday
Green eggs and ham	Lobster		Lambchops	Fish & Chips	FREE DAY	Bag of doritos

Now, let's make that menu a little taller. Right-click, "select table properties," and check off "Minimum row height." I'll make it one inch. This means if the text is longer, it could be more than 1 inch, but it will be at least one inch:

Dimensions (inches)

☐ Column width

☑ Minimum row height   1

Cell padding   0.069

Table alignment

Center ▾

Left indent (inches)   0

Sunday	Monday	Tuesday	Wednesday	Thursday	Friday	Saturday
Green eggs and ham	Lobster		Lambchops	Fish & Chips	FREE DAY	Bag of doritos

We almost have the menu where we want it, but there's still a little work to be done. Let's make the cells show the text in the middle of the cell. Go to "Table properties" and under "Cell Vertical Alignment," select "middle":

Cell vertical alignment

Top

Middle

Bottom

Now everything is evenly aligned in the middle:

Sunday	Monday	Tuesday	Wednesday	Thursday	Friday	Saturday
Green eggs and ham	Lobster		Lambchops	Fish & Chips	FREE DAY	Bag of doritos

Right now, all the columns are the same width. You can make the table larger by dragging either end of the table:

Sunday	Monday	Tuesday	Wednesday	Thursday	Friday	Saturday
Green eggs and ham	Lobster		Lambchops	Fish & Chips	FREE DAY	Bag of doritos

HOW TO INSERT SPREADSHEETS FROM GOOGLE SHEET

Google Docs integrates all things Google into it. Let's take that to heart and look at another Google app quickly: Google Sheets.

Go ahead and go back to drive.google.com and create a new document—this time a spreadsheet (hint: click the new button and then select spreadsheet)

In a flash you have a spreadsheet in the cloud. All the menus are pretty similar to Google Docs, and you enter text the same way.

For this example, I'm going to use a library database that's already been created. Let's pretend I want to copy some of it (though I could also do all of it) into my Google Doc. I just need to highlight what I want to copy, then either right-click and choose "copy" or do CTRL-C on the keyboard.

Next, I'll go back into my Google Doc and hit CTRL-V on the keyboard to paste it. It's going to ask us if we want to paste it in Linked or unlinked:

Paste table

⦿ Link to spreadsheet

Only editors can update the table. Collaborators can see a link to the source spreadsheet.

◯ Paste unlinked

Learn more   Cancel   Paste

What's the difference? Linked lets a person go to that original spreadsheet—they can view other rows and make changes. Unlinked pastes it in as a new table and if you make changes to the spreadsheet, it won't show up in your Google Doc.

I'm going to pick Linked. It will paste in and look pretty…basic:

A brief history of time	Stephen W. Hawking	Hawking, Stephen W.	Bantam Books		Astronomy	198	QB981 .H377 1988
A Career as an Electrician	Daniel E. Harmon	Harmon, Daniel E.	The Rosen Publishing Group, Inc	2010	Juvenile Nonfiction	80	TK159 .H37 2011
A Child's Garden of Verses	Robert Louis Stevenson	Stevenson, Robert Louis	Chronicle Books	1989	Juvenile Nonfiction	30	PR548 9 .C5 1989
A Concise Guide to Technical Communication	Laura J. Gurak, John M. Lannon	Gurak, Laura J.	Pearson/Longman	2004	Technology & Engineering	17	T10.5 .G83
A Concise Public Speaking Handbook	Steven A. Beebe, Susan J. Beebe	Beebe, Steven A.	Allyn & Bacon		Performing Arts	292	PN412 9.15 .B42 2012
					Techno		TK786

Just like the table we created earlier, however, you can go in and create all sorts of styles for it. For example, I chose "table property" and changed the background color for the first two rows:

These changes don't show up in the original spreadsheet.

So let's pretend that you also linked your sheet into Google Docs. If you click on the link button in the upper corner, then you'll get new options:

You can unlink the document, for example, or open it. If sharing is not turned on, the other person won't be able to access it.

THERE'S A TEMPLATE FOR THAT

Once you know your way around Google Docs, you can save time by using one of the pre-created Google Templates for Docs. To use one, go to drive.google.com and create a Google Doc—but instead of blank, select from template.

A new window is going to open with all of your options. Unlike Word and Pages, Google isn't huge on templates, but they do allow others to add templates, and you can find plenty of others by doing a quick Google search for Google Docs templates.

TABLE OF CONTENTS

One useful feature is the table of contents. This would more commonly be used in a book or long-form document. You hopefully won't use it to share a love letter with your wife, but you might want to use it if you are using Google Docs for a dissertation.

You can see/add the table of contents by going to Insert > Table of contents. You can do it either with or without the page numbers:

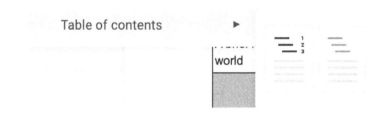

If you don't see your table of contents after adding it, there's likely a good reason: you haven't added any headings to the Doc.

Click on Normal text from your drop down. See all the different options?

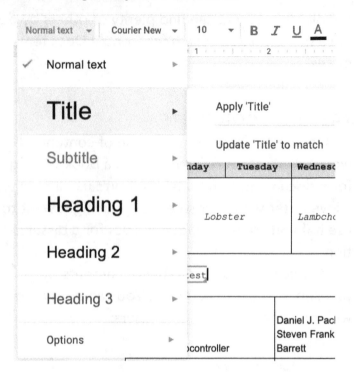

If this were a book, then "Title" would be the title on the first page. "Heading 1" would be the chapter title, "Heading 2" and "Heading 3" would be sections within that chapter.

For each one you can select "Update 'Title' to match." Let's say "Title" changes the text to size 24 but you want it to be size 36. If you change your text to size 36, then highlight it and select "Title" and update it. Then, every time you add a new Title in the doc (not other docs) it will update it to that style.

If you want it to apply to every doc going forward, then go to "Options" in that same section and select "Save as my default styles":

Options	▶	Save as my default styles
		Use my default styles
		Reset styles

THIS AND THAT

> This chapter will cover:
> * Google Docs menus

In this section, I'll cover some final things you need to know about Google Docs. This isn't comprehensive—I'm not going to cover Script Editor, for example, because the point is to keep things simple and show you the features you'll most likely be using.

File menu

We've covered all the important things in the file menu, but there's one thing of note: File > Language:

By default, it will be in English; that means if you start typing a document in Spanish, then you'll see all kinds of grammatical errors. Changing the language adds in a new dictionary so it doesn't think you are just typing gibberish.

View Menu

There are two things I'll point out under the View menu. First, Print layout. By default, it's checked off. Clicking it will show the document in a long scroll view—so no page breaks:

View   Insert   Form:

Print layout

"Show document online" will bring up a side panel to show all the headers in your document:

✓ Show document outline   Ctrl+⌘A Ctrl+⌘H

Insert Menu

If you want to add a header (such as every page has your last name on top), or add in page number, then head to "Insert" and "Header & page number."

Insert > Break will add in a page break. By default, Google does this automatically, but if you are doing a new section that you want on a new page, then you can do it manually here:

Insert > Special characters is where you can grab symbols like the © sign:

Ω Special characters

Insert > Bookmark is helpful in longer documents. You can create bookmark links, so whenever you are referencing something, you can send them right to that section so they don't have to scroll to find it:

Bookmark

Tools Menu

The tools menu is where you'll find Spell checker and word count.

Tools   Add-ons   Help   All changes saved in Drive

Spelling and grammar   ▶

Word count   ⌘+Shift+C

You can also see the built in dictionary and where you can translate the document into another language. I should note here that this is obviously a computer translation, so don't expect perfection.

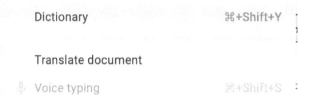

Dictionary   ⌘+Shift+Y

Translate document

🎤 Voice typing   ⌘+Shift+S

"Explore" is helpful in research papers. It keeps you in the doc so you don't have to go to a tab to look something up:

⭐ Explore   ⌘+Option+Shift+I

In the below example, I typed in "Stephen Colbert" and it gave me basic information about him in a side menu:

Add-ons Menu

This is where you can add on extensions if you don't go to the Google store:

Add-ons Help All change

Document add-ons

Get add-ons

Manage add-ons

I

Help Menu

And finally, the help menu will let you search for common tasks, see updates to Google Docs, and even get training:

Help All changes saved in Drive

Search the menus (Option+/)

Docs Help

Training

Updates

Report a problem

Report abuse/copyright

⌨ Keyboard shortcuts ⌘/

GOOGLE DOCS KEYBOARD SHORTCUTS

You can see all the keyboard shortcuts in Google Docs by selecting Help > Keyboard shortcuts.

For your reference, below are some of the most common ones you'll use.

Common actions	
Copy	**Ctrl + c**
Cut	**Ctrl + x**
Paste	**Ctrl + v**
Paste without formatting	**Ctrl + Shift + v**
Undo	**Ctrl + z**
Redo	**Ctrl + Shift + z**
Insert or edit link	**Ctrl + k**
Print	**Ctrl + p**
Open	**Ctrl + o**
Find	**Ctrl + f**
Find and replace	**Ctrl + h**
Text formatting	
Bold	**Ctrl + b**
Italicize	**Ctrl + i**
Underline	**Ctrl + u**
Strikethrough	**Alt + Shift + 5**
Superscript	**Ctrl + .**
Subscript	**Ctrl + ,**
Copy text formatting	**Ctrl + Alt + c**

Paste text formatting	**Ctrl + Alt + v**
Clear text formatting	**Ctrl + **
Increase font size	**Ctrl + Shift + >**
Decrease font size	**Ctrl + Shift + <**

Paragraph formatting

Increase paragraph indentation	**Ctrl +]**
Decrease paragraph indentation	**Ctrl + [**
Apply normal text style	**Ctrl + Alt + 0**
Apply heading style [1-6]	**Ctrl + Alt + [1-6]**
Left align	**Ctrl + Shift + l**
Center align	**Ctrl + Shift + e**
Right align	**Ctrl + Shift + r**
Justify	**Ctrl + Shift + j**
Numbered list	**Ctrl + Shift + 7**
Bulleted list	**Ctrl + Shift + 8**

Comments

Insert comment	**Ctrl + Alt + m**
Open discussion thread	**Ctrl + Alt + Shift + a**

Menus

File menu	**Alt + f**
Edit menu	**Alt + e**
View menu	**Alt + v**
Insert menu	**Alt + i**
Format menu	**Alt + o**
Tools menu	**Alt + t**
Help menu	**Alt + h**

INDEX

ABOUT THE AUTHOR

Scott La Counte is a librarian and writer. His first book, *Quiet, Please: Dispatches from a Public Librarian* (Da Capo 2008) was the editor's choice for the Chicago Tribune and a Discovery title for the Los Angeles Times; in 2011, he published the YA book The N00b Warriors, which became a #1 Amazon bestseller; his most recent book is *#OrganicJesus: Finding Your Way to an Unprocessed, GMO-Free Christianity* (Kregel 2016).

He has written dozens of best-selling how-to guides on tech products.

You can connect with him at ScottDouglas.org.